OFF TO A GOOD START

A Behaviorally Based Model
for Teaching Children with
Down Syndrome

Book 1: Foundations for Learning

Emily A. Jones, PhD, BCBA-D, and
Kathleen M. Feeley, PhD

WOODBINE HOUSE

Library of Congress Cataloging-in-Publication Data

Names: Feeley, Kathleen M., author.
Title: Off to a good start : a behaviorally based model for teaching children
  with down syndrome / Kathleen M. Feeley and Emily A. Jones.
Description: Bethesda, MD : Woodbine House, [2018] | Includes
bibliographical references and index. |
Identifiers: LCCN 2018000537 (print) | LCCN 2018000736 (ebook) | ISBN
  9781606132623 (book 1) | ISBN 9781606132883 (book 2) | ISBN 9781606132616
  (book 1) | ISBN 9781606132876 (book 2)
Subjects: LCSH: Down syndrome. | Children with mental
  disabilities--Education. | Children with mental disabilities--Care. | Child rearing.
Classification: LCC RJ506.D68 (ebook) | LCC RJ506.D68 F44 2018 (print) |
DDC   649/.1528--dc2
LC record available at https://lccn.loc.gov/2018000537

We dedicate this manual to the children with Down syndrome with whom we have had the absolute pleasure of spending time and to their families who entrusted us with their darlings. The generosity of these families and their willingness to be pioneers in this region with respect to not only the type of intervention but also to their pursuit of inclusive programming is astounding.

ACKNOWLEDGMENTS

This manual is the culmination of twenty years of work integrating our knowledge about applied behavior analysis with the phenotypic characteristics of Down syndrome. It began with the influence of our esteemed mentors, Dr. Joe Reichle and the late Dr. Edward Carr, who taught us to be scientists and provided tremendous support for this work. We have also learned from the researchers across the globe who share a particular interest in Down syndrome and are dedicated to disseminating their findings.

Our work also reflects relationships with professionals who were open to trying our approach and who provided us with guidance before long. To them and the many students who have been a part of the research and clinical work on which this manual is based, and whose expertise helped inform early materials for this book, we are especially thankful.

We also extend our appreciation to our editor, Susan Stokes, whose input was invaluable, and to Woodbine House publishers for their dedication to enhancing the lives of individuals with disabilities through parent- and practitioner-focused books.

Importantly, we want to thank our families. Without their support, we could not have written this manual. We thank our children, particularly Emily's young Jacob and Allison, who tolerated less time with their moms so that this manual could come to fruition. And we thank our husbands, who have tirelessly and patiently picked up the slack when so much of our time and energy was diverted to this project.

A special thank-you to those who have generously contributed to this manual:

- Sara Bauer, PhD, BCBA-D, Licensed Behavior Analyst, New York, Lecturer, Queens College, City University of New York, shared her expertise and assistance in developing Chapter 2.
- Alysha Rafeeq, BA, Queens College and the Graduate Center, City University of New York, shared her expertise and assistance in developing material for Chapter 3.
- Holly Weisberg, MA, BCBA, Licensed Behavior Analyst, New York, Queens College and the Graduate Center, City University of New York, shared her expertise and assistance in developing material for Chapter 3.
- Nicole Blach, Catherine Kelly, and Hannah Speigel took countless photos for this book. Their flexibility, patience, and dedication were invaluable.

TABLE OF CONTENTS

Chapter 1

OUR JOURNEY

On July 31, 1998, a baby was born with an extra 21st chromosome. Owen Michael Kelly was the first child with Down syndrome with whom we had the opportunity to implement the interventions described in this manual. We were both working toward our PhDs with mentors who were leading behavior analysts in their respective fields (Dr. Joe Reichle from the University of Minnesota and the late Dr. Edward Carr from the State University of New York, Stony Brook). And we had both just accepted positions offered to us by Mike Darcy, the founding director of a preschool program that used intensive behavior analytic interventions with children with autism spectrum disorders (a disorder in brain development resulting in difficulties in social interaction and communication along with repetitive

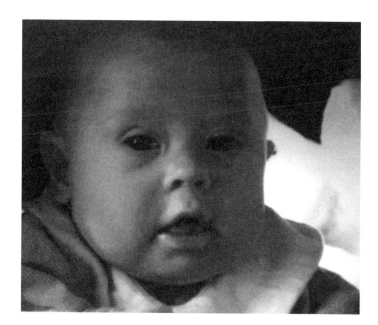

behavior). We were hired to extend that program to even younger children with autism, from diagnosis through three years of age.

As we developed interventions for the children with autism, we tried using the very same strategies with Owen. Lo and behold, the interventions were not only incredibly effective for the children with autism, but for Owen as well.

Two years later, thanks to Mike Darcy, we had the opportunity to start a program for children with Down syndrome in our region. This allowed us to replicate the strategies we had implemented with Owen with several other children. Since then, we have dedicated a large part of our careers to developing and demonstrating the effectiveness of these interventions; seventeen years later we made the commitment to publish this comprehensive manual.

Where Did We Start?

We started by scouring the research conducted with children with Down syndrome up until that time. We will talk more about research in Chapter 2, but for now, let's just say we tried to get our hands on every research article in which an intervention was systematically tested to see if it improved some aspect of development in children with Down syndrome (e.g., their speech, motor skills, etc.). In reviewing the research that had been conducted up until 1998, we found articles from the 1960s and 1970s demonstrating the effectiveness of interventions with children with Down syndrome. This early research showed that strategies utilizing what is referred to as *applied behavior analysis* were effective; that is, the strategies improved some aspect of development.

For those unfamiliar with the term *applied behavior analysis,* simply stated, it refers to interventions that systematically change what comes before a desired behavior and/or what follows that behavior to improve the behavior. A simple example is that every time a six-month-old baby makes a speech sound, his parents make sure they talk to and even tickle her, and the baby's speech sounds increase.

We were quite familiar with applied behavior analysis, as it was the basis for much of our work before we became specifically interested in children with Down syndrome. You see, the principles of applied behavior analysis (ABA) were, and continue to be, at the very foundation of many interventions designed to improve a variety of outcomes for individuals, including those with disabilities. For example, research has demonstrated that behavior analytic interventions improve children's reading, math, self-care (e.g., tooth brushing, dressing), social, and communication skills. In 1998, its use was increasingly expanding to meet the needs of children with autism. Very important and influential research papers were being published demonstrating the positive impact that applied behavior analysis had on the development of children with autism. It just made sense that we could apply these interventions with children with Down syndrome to achieve similar success.

The research examining applied behavior analysis with children with Down syndrome we did find had an odd trend. In the 1960s and 1970s, some studies had demonstrated that by systematically changing consequences and presenting multiple teaching opportunities (one right after the other), children with Down syndrome acquired a large number of skills. This was very promising. But, then, the research *focusing* on interventions specifically for children with Down syndrome seemed to stop. Intervention research did continue, but with only one or two children with Down syndrome mixed in with other children who had different disabilities. Thus, the researchers were not necessarily concentrating on the specific needs of children with Down syndrome as they examined the effectiveness of a particular intervention.

So what was the focus of researchers who were specifically interested in Down syndrome at that time? It was descriptive. This means studies were conducted to carefully examine how children with Down syndrome performed and progressed in the absence of any specific intervention designed to influence their performance. This research was just as important; it told us how children with Down syndrome spoke, walked, played, etc.—that is, about their characteristics. This work showed how children with Down syndrome developed in similar ways as children who were typically developing. It also showed how their development was delayed in comparison to typical development. Then, researchers began to carefully examine how children with specific disabilities, particularly those associated with a chromosome disorder, such as Down syndrome, were more likely to develop differently than typically developing children and even *differently* than children with other disabilities.

An understanding of these similarities and differences in development led to the identification of the ***Down syndrome behavioral phenotype.*** Behavioral phenotype refers to the increased likelihood that a child with a given disorder (e.g., Down syndrome) will show certain characteristic behaviors, both strengths and weaknesses (Dykens, 1995). It describes behaviors that one might observe. This is in contrast to the ***Down syndrome genotype,*** which refers to the actual genetic makeup of children with Down syndrome (the presence of an extra copy of the twenty-first chromosome). The research showed that individuals with Down syndrome are likely to show relatively strong social interest, language comprehension (receptive language), and visual processing abilities—skills that enable them to understand and learn from what they see. At the same time, individuals with Down syndrome are likely to have weaker auditory processing skills and poorer speech and expressive language skills, along with specific difficulties in certain areas of cognitive and motor development.

Research about the Down syndrome behavioral phenotype was of particular interest to us. With knowledge of specific characteristics, we were confident we could develop interventions that built upon the strengths associated with the Down syndrome behavioral phenotype to specifically address the weaknesses. This approach to intervention is referred to as *etiology-based intervention* and in 1998 had yet to be applied to children with Down syndrome.

● ● ● ● ● ● ● ● ● ● ● ●

Our Model

With knowledge of the research providing evidence for behavior analytic interventions and knowledge of the Down syndrome behavioral phenotype, we developed this behaviorally based model of intervention that we share with you here. We have designed this two-part manual to provide you—the parents, grandparents, teachers, and other service providers and caregivers of young children with Down syndrome—with the following:

- an understanding of the characteristic strengths and weaknesses associated with the Down syndrome behavioral phenotype
- a rationale, supported by research, for using interventions that are based on the principles of applied behavior analysis
- an understanding of the basic principles of applied behavior analysis and how they can be systematically used to enhance the acquisition of skills in young children with Down syndrome while simultaneously decreasing behaviors that interfere with learning
- accounts of families' experiences using this approach with their young children with Down syndrome
- a curriculum that can be used to guide intervention that builds upon relative strengths and specifically addresses characteristic weaknesses in young children with Down syndrome. This curriculum addresses five essential areas of development:
  - ➤ motor development
  - ➤ social-communication development
  - ➤ cognitive development
  - ➤ self-care skills
  - ➤ behavior that interferes with learning
- step-by-step procedures for teaching skills in each area of development
- an understanding of how to put this intervention in place for your child while at the same time ensuring your child's access to your community

Navigating This Two-Part Manual

This manual has been published in two books to meet the unique needs of our readers. Some readers will likely have a strong background in applied behavior analysis and implementing behaviorally based interventions. Thus, they may be quite familiar with much of the background information in Book 1 and only need Book 2 to implement the programs with children with Down syndrome. However, a large number of readers may be unfamiliar with all or most of the background content in Book 1 and would benefit from having both Books 1 and 2.

Now, to get the most of this manual, we suggest you set aside time to read through this introductory chapter about our journey and the following chapter, which provides an overview of the Down syndrome behavioral phenotype and a brief review of the research related to intervention strategies. This is particularly important to share with any professionals (e.g., educator, speech-language pathologist, physical therapist, etc.) providing services to your child. If the professionals on your team are not familiar with the perspective this manual reflects, the information in Chapter 2 will be a good introduction.

In Chapter 3 of this book we provide an overview of the basic principles of behavior analytic interventions that have been demonstrated effective in the research literature reviewed in Chapter 2. This is one of our favorite chapters, as we have the opportunity to explain potentially complicated intervention strategies in a way that we hope you will understand and then easily apply with your child with Down syndrome. Chapter 3 also includes many definitions of terms and discusses how they influence your child's performance. The terms are defined and described through three stories of young children with Down syndrome whose programs and progress we will continue to document throughout the manual. We also use everyday examples (outside of teaching young children with Down syndrome) to help you gain a better understanding of the concepts. You see, the principles of learning that influence the behavior of young children with Down syndrome actually influence all of our behavior. We suggest you refer back to Chapter 3 often as you make your way through this manual. Having written this manual for both family members and professionals, we are acutely aware that the skill level within both groups is quite vast. Thus, while keeping the manual user friendly, we have added more technical information, called **Advanced Information,** for those who are interested in expanding their knowledge.

Chapter 4 in this book focuses on working with the service delivery system in your community and accessing additional resources to create interventions for your child. Finally, in Chapter 5, families describe their stories using this model. We have selected these families based on their range of experiences, so it is likely many of you will be presented with the same accomplishments and challenges they faced. Appendix A includes the forms you will need to understand the basics of setting up and monitoring this intervention with your child and Appendix B offers a wealth of related resources you will likely find helpful as you implement these interventions. The references are sources we consulted in writing both Book 1 and Book 2.

Book 2 is dedicated to the instructional programs to teach your child from birth to kindergarten (five or six years of age). In the first chapter of Book 2, we discuss setting up your child's intervention programs and determining which skills to teach him* first. You might consider this chapter the *road map* you will follow as you implement the behavior analytic strategies introduced in Chapter 3 of this book.

In Chapters 2–5 of Book 2, we discuss motor, cognitive, social-communication, and self-care development as well as behavior that interferes with learning. Each chapter corresponds to a developmental period. We describe intervention programs for skills that are part of the Down syndrome behavioral phenotype or are foundational for learning. For each skill, we map out an intervention program that includes the following:

- a rationale for addressing the skill
- a skill sequence that breaks the skill into teachable targets
- steps for teaching
- **Helpful Hints** with additional information to help you tailor the intervention to your child and family
- case examples describing strategies to teach the skill
- a Progress Tracker to make notes about your child's progress learning the skills

At the end of each of these chapters, we discuss accessing the community. In this section, we define and describe important aspects of early intervention, preschool services, and the special education process, focusing on access to activities and services with your child's typically developing peers. All the program sheets and progress tracker templates needed to help you implement the interventions with your child with Down syndrome are included in the appendix of Book 2.

. . . .

Where Is Owen Now?

So, you may be wondering what happened to that baby, Owen Michael Kelly. Well, we can remember as if it were yesterday his father saying, "Owen will be given the same opportunities as his older brothers, in *all* aspects of life." At the time, his brothers were one and three years of age. Owen *has* had the same opportunities as his brothers. He attended the same schools and had the same teachers as his brothers (and his younger sister) and participated in the same sports and recreational ac-

---

* Male pronouns are used to refer to the child with Down syndrome in odd-numbered chapters and female pronouns are used in even-numbered chapters.

tivities. And at this moment, he just wrapped up his first semester at a specially designed program on the campus of a state university that just happens to be in his neighborhood.

Now, there were a few components of Owen's program that were and continue to be essential to his success. As described in this manual, his instruction has always been based on the principles of applied behavior analysis. Also, goals were identified based on his specific strengths and weaknesses. For example, Owen has always found reading challenging, so an hour each day was and still is dedicated to reading instruction. His continued challenges with speech and language skills were also addressed daily, in-

cluding through a public speaking class in his high school right alongside his typically developing peers. Within his college program, supported by his school district's personnel, he creates and gives speeches to share his life experiences within classes throughout the university.

Owen's strengths have always been his social skills. The very first year of preschool, his teacher said, "The children love to be around Owen. They enjoy his company and love to play with him." This continues to be true, as throughout high school he was a member of the student council, the fishing club, and the senior prom committee, and he was the valued manager of his high school's varsity lacrosse team. Currently, he works in the equipment room at his university, which gives him a prominent position on the sidelines at all sporting events.

Owen continues to be an avid bicyclist and card player, and, as his brothers describe, "He rocks at Madden Sport [a video game]!" With his family's commitment and the interventions described in this manual, beginning when Owen was born and continuing to this day nineteen years later, it is clear that Owen has had the same opportunities as his siblings and truly is meeting his full potential.

Chapter 2

OUR MODEL

Now that you have an idea of how we started this journey, we will provide you with an overview of the foundations of our model for intervention. The first is targeting skills identified as areas of weakness characteristic of children with Down syndrome. The second is using evidence-based interventions grounded in applied behavior analysis to build upon strengths typically demonstrated by children with Down syndrome (i.e., phenotypic strengths). The third is providing intervention alongside typically developing peers. Let's consider each of these foundations of our model in more detail.

WHAT SKILLS DO WE NEED TO TEACH?

The answer to this question lies in an understanding of the strengths and weaknesses characteristic of children with Down syndrome. Remember, we introduced this pattern of strengths and weaknesses and the term **behavioral phenotype** in Chapter 1 of this book. *Behavioral phenotype* refers to the increased probability that individuals with a certain disorder (in this case, Down syndrome) show certain characteristics (Dykens, 1995). For example, individuals with Down syndrome are likely to show relatively strong social interest but poorer expressive communication skills. This does not mean everyone with Down syndrome will show each of the characteristics, nor to the same degree, but it is more likely that your child with Down syndrome will show these phenotypic characteristics.

Keep in mind that strengths and weaknesses are relative. This means an area might be considered a strength if a given child performs better than we would expect of children the same age in years and months (chronological age). For example, for many children with Down syndrome, social skills are a relative strength in that they are similar to, and sometimes even better than, those of typically developing children of the same age—something you may already know if you have spent time with children with Down syndrome. An area might also be considered a strength if a child performs better than expected given her overall skill level (usually some measure of intelligence). Another way to view an area of strength is if a child performs better in that area in comparison to her performance in another specific skill area. For example, the ability to understand what other people say is a relative strength in children with Down syndrome compared to the ability to express themselves through speech.

The same comparisons can be made for weaknesses, areas in which children do not perform as well as we would expect. Weakness may be delays, meaning children with Down syndrome will develop the skill, but it will take longer than it does for typically developing children. Weaknesses may also consist of deficits, meaning children with Down syndrome show differences in the way they develop those skills or do not develop the skills at all. For example, early motor development is delayed, but there are also some differences in the ways infants and young children with Down syndrome move their bodies compared to typically developing children.

It is important to realize that strengths and weaknesses change as children grow. For example, a social strength observed in infants with Down syndrome (in comparison to typically developing infants) is that they look at their caregivers more than they look at toys. This same social strength may also be seen later when children with Down syndrome develop peer relationships that qualify as true friendships.

We owe the extensive understanding of the Down syndrome behavioral phenotype and critical areas of need to the many researchers who have conducted this work over the past several decades. They have described the behavioral phenotype by observing large numbers of children with Down syndrome and comparing how they learn to typically developing children and to children with intellectual disabilities due to unknown causes or other syndromes (e.g., Williams syndrome or fragile X syndrome). Jennifer Wishart and her colleagues in Scotland conducted much of the early work. Here in the United States, Robert Hodapp, Elizabeth Dykens, Lynn Nadel, Deborah Fidler, and their colleagues have contributed significantly to our understanding of the Down syndrome behavioral phenotype. This research literature is extensive. In the next section, we describe some of what they have learned in more detail, discussing each of the areas of development that we focus on in this manual.

● ●

The Down Syndrome Behavioral Phenotype

You have probably already learned a bit about the characteristics of the Down syndrome behavioral phenotype. So some of this will sound familiar to you. You can probably identify some of the characteristics in your own child. And you may already be seeing how your child's rate of development is variable, with some areas delayed, some showing impairments, and some showing relative strength.

Motor Development

Motor development refers to how a child acquires and refines skills that involve moving her body. It includes movements of the head, trunk, arms, legs, and finer movements of the fingers and facial muscles. Motor development is one area in which children with Down syndrome show both weaknesses and strengths. In later childhood, gross motor skills such as running speed and agility, along with coordinating visual information with motor skills such as looking carefully while catching a ball (referred to as visual motor control), all seem to be areas of strength. That is, children with Down syndrome may be able to perform these skills as well as, or almost as well as, same-age typical peers. However, young children with Down syndrome show delays in progressing through the stages of motor development, and beginning in infancy, there are already delays and differences.

Infants with Down syndrome also make atypical movement patterns (such as propping the head on the upper back while lying on their stomachs) that may negatively affect motor development. Delays and differences may be more evident toward the end of the first year of life, especially as children begin to stand and walk and face more complex skills. Sometimes gross motor movements are slower and less efficient, especially with more complicated skills such as walking and balancing on something. In fine motor tasks (those that require skilled use of fingers and hands), movements may be quicker but less accurate.

Hypotonia and hyperflexibility are common characteristics of children with Down syndrome that affect motor development. *Hypotonia* refers to low muscle tone. Muscle tone can be compared to pasta (yes, pasta!). An uncooked piece of spaghetti could be described as having much tone (thus, a great deal of tension) and a well-cooked piece of spaghetti as having very little tone. When muscles have low tone, they tend to be less tense. Hypotonia may result in a child seeming "floppy," with her arms and legs hanging and/or poor head control.

Hyperflexibility refers to excessive range of movement and extension of the joints. Ligaments are made of connective tissue, and their role is to connect one bone to another at the joint. This connective tissue is typically tight. But, children with Down syndrome have a tendency to have loose ligaments, which may result in abnormal range of motion. This means your baby may move her arms and legs in ways most of us cannot, and her hips may rotate outward. Both hypotonia and hyperflexibility have a tremendous impact on the way children with Down syndrome do many things, including roll over, crawl, and walk.

In 2001, Valentine Dmitriev, an educator and researcher at one of the first early intervention programs for children with Down syndrome, described four patterns of muscle tone and motor skills in infants with Down syndrome. A small percentage of children with Down syndrome (15–25 percent) show good muscle tone and meet

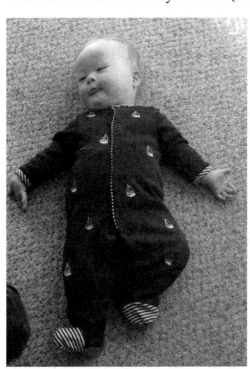

early motor milestones such as head control in the typical time frame. A large portion (50–60 percent) fall into one of two types characterized by a discrepancy between the upper and lower body; some have strong upper bodies but very weak lower bodies, and others, the opposite pattern. A final, small percentage of babies (15–25 percent) show all-over weakness, often along with cardiovascular problems. Physical therapist Patricia Winders has also described children with Down syndrome as showing differences in motivation to engage in motor behavior, some seeking to practice motor movements and others content to watch (Winders, 2014). The observations of Dmitriev and Winders suggest that children with Down syndrome may be very different from each other in their motor development.

Hypotonia and hyperflexibility also affect movement patterns (the way children move their bodies). For example, low tone and loose ligaments may result in a baby's hips rotating outward, which in turn leads the child to walk with a wide base. When sitting, your child may spread her legs extremely far apart and then drop her body forward (between her legs) to get into a crawling position, stretching her ligaments even further. This can have negative effects on later walking skills.

These differences make it more difficult for children with Down syndrome to achieve early-developing skills such as sitting and walking as well as reaching and grasping things in their environment and later-developing activities such as riding a bike or scooter and playing soccer. In fact, the first area of motor development to address is working and developing your child's muscles just by having her lie in different positions. Being on her back, side, and tummy helps your baby practice head and upper body control and develop the muscles necessary for later motor skills such as walking, running, and jumping.

Motor planning, or *praxis*, refers to your child's ability to plan movements to complete a task. Even in toddlers, motor planning is associated with how well children participate in daily activities, such as using utensils and manipulating toys. Motor planning is often an area of difficulty for children with Down syndrome. For example, infants with Down syndrome may have trouble reaching in a straight line toward something, suggesting a deficit in organizing the movements needed to reach. Children and adults continue to show difficulty in motor planning, including making precise limb and finger movements such as those required for dressing skills and handwriting.

So far we have focused on motor development in terms of movements of the arms, legs, hands, etc., and the effects of hypotonia and hyperflexibility. But, motor development also involves control of the movements of the parts of the mouth, face, and jaw, referred to as **oral motor skills**. There are many muscles in the mouth and face, and decreased tone and muscle weakness affect these muscles

just like any other muscles in the body. Differences in oral motor skills common in children with Down syndrome include tongue protrusion, atypical tongue movements, problems with lip closure, and poor jaw control. Children also may have physical differences (e.g., the mouth is smaller). Oral motor skills are important for speech development as well as self-care skills such as drinking and eating.

Social-Communication Development

Social-communication refers broadly to how your child interacts with others. This includes understanding what others are saying and understanding social conventions (e.g., when to shake hands versus wave) and expressing her wants and needs.

Social development is a relative strength for children with Down syndrome. Children tend to be socially competent and socially interested, forming true friendships and showing even more empathy than children with other types of developmental disabilities. In infancy, babies with Down syndrome look longer at their mothers than typically developing babies do and engage in more play acts, turn taking, and *joint attention* (sharing attention with another person in relation to an interesting object).

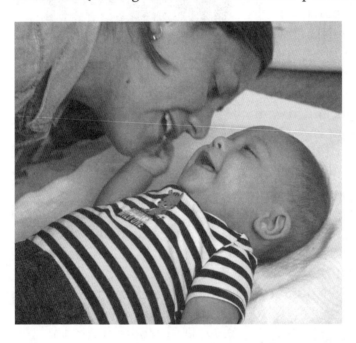

Your child may even smile more. However, one characteristic that can go along with this relative sophistication in social skills and social interest is the overuse (or inappropriate use) of social skills in certain situations (e.g., hugging strangers).

While social development is a relative strength, you have probably heard that communication is an area of much more difficulty for children with Down syndrome. For many parents, one of their biggest concerns is their child's development of communication skills. And rightly so—your child's ability to express her wants and needs is a critical piece of successful interaction and learning.

Communication is a broad term involving several different aspects. Your child already communicates with you in some ways to let you know what she needs and wants. The social use or function of speech and language is referred to as *pragmatics. Language* refers to a system of words or symbols used to communicate in a given community (e.g., an English- or Spanish-speaking community) and includes rules for the meaning of words, making new words, and putting words together. *Speech* involves using one's voice to produce sounds and words and requires the coordination of many systems of the brain, as well as the strength, coordination, and timing of muscle movements. In fact, it is speech you are probably thinking most about when you think about your child's communication skills.

Pragmatics

Pragmatics is generally a strength for children with Down syndrome, who usually express their social interest by communicating and interacting. But, heightened social interest may also mean some pragmatic aspects of communication can be difficult, such as learning how to appropriately interact with strangers, acquaintances, friends, and family. Each of these groups calls for a different type of social interaction, as you would not greet a complete stranger with a hug and a kiss, nor would you shake hands and introduce yourself to a close family member.

Children with Down syndrome already start to show differences in pragmatics skills within the first year of life. For example, compared to typically developing children, young children with Down syndrome often show impaired nonverbal *requesting*, that is, communicating without the use of words to get their needs met—for example, looking or pointing to indicate hunger, discomfort, or a desire for a toy that fell out of reach.

Using gestures (e.g., pointing, showing) is actually a relative strength in children with Down syndrome. And children with Down syndrome are good at using gestures to engage in social interactions by drawing other people's attention to interesting things (referred to as joint attention). But often, children with Down syndrome are not as skilled at using these same gestures to request (e.g., pointing to get a toy on a high shelf). The issue here is the *reason* children are pointing. Poor requesting and better joint attention may relate to an overall lower level of interest in objects such as toys and things in the environment (referred to as *object interest*) and a heightened interest in interacting with others (i.e., social interest). This means your child is more likely to communicate or engage in behaviors to get your attention than to gain access to an object. It is not that objects are not interesting; rather, in comparison to social consequences, the objects may not be *as* motivating.

Language

Expressive language refers to your child's ability to share her thoughts, ideas, and feelings. By the time children with Down syndrome are three years of age, expressive language usually falls behind overall cognitive ability by at least six months. It is also delayed compared to other children's expressive language skills and their own receptive language skills. By *receptive language* we mean your child's understanding of language (e.g., pointing to a cat in a book when asked, "Where's the cat?"). Children with Down syndrome tend to have receptive language skills consistent with their overall level of cognitive functioning, but it is likely still delayed compared to typically developing children of the same age. The majority of children with Down syndrome under five years of age already show this pattern of relatively stronger receptive than expressive language skills. With age, the number of children who have this discrepancy increases and the gap between receptive and expressive language continues to grow.

Growth in *vocabulary* (word meanings) is likely to be relatively steady, although first spoken words usually occur later than usual. Around eighteen months of age, typically developing children experience a vocabulary spurt or sudden expansion in the number of words they use and understand. For children with Down syndrome, this vocabulary spurt usually occurs around three years of age. Though vocabulary is delayed compared to chronological age, a child's vocabulary may be as good as, or better than, we would expect given her overall level of cognitive functioning. Given the discrepancy between receptive and expressive language, you can probably guess that your child will likely be able to understand much more vocabulary than she can express and her vocabulary will continue to grow into adulthood. So...be very careful when you are communicating things that you *don't* want your child to hear!

As your child's vocabulary grows, she will begin to put words together. *Grammar* or *syntax* refers to the rules in a language about the order of words in sentences (e.g., in the English language, nouns tend to come before verbs as in, "The cat [noun] ran [verb]."). *Morphology* refers to parts of words (*morphemes*) such as verb tense endings (e.g., "ed," "ing"), plurals, and possessives (e.g., "the cat's mitten"). Sometimes these areas together are referred to as *morphosyntax*. Children with Down syndrome show delays in producing multiword utterances, which may be related not only to vocabulary, but also to difficulties with grammar or morphosyntactic development.

In typical development, children do not start to follow grammatical rules such as the possessive *s*, plurals, and verb tenses until they have 200 to 250 spontaneous words. Although children with Down syndrome make steady progress in vocabulary growth, they are typically delayed at getting to that 250-word mark, which is one reason we see delays in the development of grammar.

Speech

The overall number of sounds a baby with Down syndrome makes, the age when she begins to make specific sounds, and the characteristics of consonants (e.g., /d/, /b/, /m/) and vowels (e.g., /a/, /e/, /i/, /o/) she produces during babbling are all similar to those of typically developing infants. Also, as you might have noticed, your baby with Down syndrome probably makes lots of nonspeech sounds (e.g., burps, hiccups, raspberries, grunts). In fact, she is likely to make more nonspeech than speech-like sounds, which is different from typically developing infants. When babies begin making speech sounds, they repeat sequences of consonant/vowel sounds (e.g., /ma/ma/ma/ or /da/da/da/). This is referred to as *canonical babbling* and is also likely delayed in infants with Down syndrome. Notice that when we refer to sounds, we place them between slashes (e.g., /ah/, /da/, and /m/) to clearly indicate we are referring to specific sounds (not letters).

Children with Down syndrome may also show delays and differences in how they practice speech sounds. For example, they are likely to have challenges repeating the exact same sound (***vocal imitation***) or word (***verbal imitation***) that someone else makes. Note that this is different from being able to imitate what your child sees (i.e., visual imitation), which is usually a relative strength for children with Down syndrome.

Another characteristic of children with Down syndrome you may have already heard about is poor articulation and intelligibility. ***Intelligibility*** has to do with how well your child's speech is understood by others. Even parents often report difficulty understanding the speech of their children with Down syndrome. Intelligibility is related to rate of speech, how much your child is trying to say, and how clearly she produces speech sounds **(*articulation*)**. Articulation refers to your child's production of the sounds of her language. Sound production is affected by physical characteristics common in children with Down syndrome such as a high, narrow palatal arch (the roof of the mouth) and a small, narrow upper jaw, which may restrict movements of the tongue. Other differences that may affect articulation include hypotonia (low tone) in the muscles of the mouth and face and a tendency to develop otitis media (ear infections), which may lead to fluctuating hearing loss.

Children with Down syndrome may also show oral motor difficulties (***dysarthria***) that make it more difficult to control and coordinate the complex oral movements for speech. When we discuss social-communication development in subsequent chapters, we will discuss these and additional variables in more detail.

Cognitive Development

Cognitive development refers to the way children acquire and use knowledge. This area of development is all about what children know as well as how they figure out the world and solve problems.

Visual Processing vs. Auditory Processing

Children with Down syndrome usually have a relative cognitive strength in processing information presented visually (i.e., things your child sees, referred to as ***visuospatial processing)***, compared to a weakness in processing information presented auditorily (i.e., things your child hears, referred to as ***auditory processing*** or ***verbal processing***). When tested, children with Down syndrome often do better when someone shows them something rather than says something. For example, children with Down syndrome may follow directions better when a caregiver shows them what to do rather than just says the instructions.

While the ability to recognize the location of an object (spatial memory) is not as strong, there are two aspects of visuospatial processing that are strengths:

- visual imitation, or imitating what one sees. Your child can likely imitate what she sees as well or almost as well as her typically developing peers.
- visual-motor integration (or eye-hand coordination), or coordinating visual information with motor actions, as in hitting a ball and using a touchscreen on a tablet.

You will begin to see how the overall pattern of better visual than auditory processing affects other developmental areas as well and can therefore be used to address weaknesses. Stronger visual processing is something we consider when developing interventions.

Executive Functions

Executive functions is one area of cognitive development that is a particular challenge for children with Down syndrome. *Executive functions* control and regulate other abilities and behaviors and include a number of skills:

- temporarily remembering something (working memory or short-term memory)
- attending to relevant information (attention)
- ignoring distracting or unimportant information (inhibition)
- shifting attention to new, relevant information (cognitive flexibility)

How quickly children process information (speed of processing), planning, and problem solving are also sometimes included in executive functions.

Now, think for a moment about the skills a child needs to succeed in school. She must pay attention to the teacher and relevant materials, ignore distracting things going on within and outside the classroom, shift attention to new information as the teacher introduces it, and hold on to information to use during the lesson, all while doing these things relatively quickly. See how executive functions are related to learning? They affect school readiness, cognitive and social-emotional development, and math and reading skills.

Children with Down syndrome experience challenges in executive functions, though this research is still emerging. We do know that children with Down syndrome show differences in the frontal lobe of the brain, the area associated with executive functions. Short-term memory, along with problem solving and planning, seem to be particularly impaired in young children, but multiple executive functions—including inhibition and shifting—may be impaired in older children and adults.

Processing speed refers to the time it takes to begin and/or complete a mental task and is also referred to as *fluency* of responding. It is measured as latency to respond (how long it takes to get started doing something) or response time (how long it takes to do something). Children and adults with Down syndrome tend to have longer response times. It is important to point out that processing speed improves over early childhood and may relate to myelination of nerves (a fatty substance that surrounds nerves and facilitates transmission of nerve impulses), something that is delayed in infants and toddlers with Down syndrome.

Because of this slower speed to respond, children with Down syndrome are often described as lacking fluency. So, when a child is asked a question, she may know how to respond but take a long time to begin and sometimes may even slowly progress through each word as she answers the question. This may make it difficult for listeners to follow the child's response, and, you can imagine, can result in the interaction breaking down (e.g., a peer may not wait for the child to answer). Processing speed and fluency affect so many skill areas, so we will discuss this throughout the book.

Slower processing speed may relate to other executive functions, including short-term memory. **Short-term memory (STM)** refers to the temporary storage of information in the brain. It is often assessed by having the person repeat back an increasingly longer series of numbers (sometimes referred to as digit span). **Working memory** refers to being able to temporarily store information in memory while doing something with that information. For example, repeating a series of numbers backward (e.g., if I say, "5, 7, 2," you would say, "2, 7, 5") involves not just storage, but also manipulating the numbers to reverse their order. Although several areas of the brain may be involved in both short- and long-term memory, the **hippocampus** is a critical structure involved in memory that is also affected by Down syndrome.

There are two types of STM:

- visual STM: for example, remembering the order of a series of blocks to recreate a tower or remembering a series of actions in a dance move you just saw
- auditory or verbal STM: for example, remembering a phone number or a list of things to get from your room after someone verbally gives you the information

So, do you think children with Down syndrome perform better on visual or auditory STM tasks? If you said visual STM, you are correct. But, in everyday interactions, your child is likely to have to remember the things she is told orally. For example, being told a list of things to get before leaving the house (e.g., Mom says, "Johnny, get your library book and the umbrella in case it rains"). Poor auditory STM can make everyday tasks and school tasks difficult. Auditory STM also affects vocabulary growth and even the length of phrases when speaking, two areas we discussed in the section on Social-Communication Development in this chapter.

Problem solving is also a critical area of executive functions for children with Down syndrome. By problem solving, we mean working on achieving a goal that cannot be attained immediately, because of some obstacle. To solve the problem, children learn rules or use strategies and then determine whether they have attained their goal. For instance, imagine that the *goal* is to obtain a ball.

	The Ball is out of reach on a blanket	the obstacle
	so the child must engage in another behavior first to get the ball	a strategy
	Success!	problem solved

The out-of-reach ball might seem like a straightforward problem, but a child needs to learn many component skills to solve it. In fact, the foundation begins when babies begin learning about objects and what objects can do (e.g., the blanket that can be pulled closer)—that is, engaging in *goal-directed actions on objects.* Once your child has learned about blankets and how they move, she might pull the blanket that the ball is on closer (strategy) and retrieve the ball. This is an example of problem solving in young children called *means-end behavior.*

Children with Down syndrome show delays and differences in these early problem-solving tasks. What children with Down syndrome generally do when presented with these types of tasks is important. They may stare at the objects without interacting with them or just disregard the objects (e.g., throw the materials off the table) and then proceed to smile and otherwise socially engage the person who presented the task. Several factors seem to be at play here. One is *task persistence* (also referred to as mastery motivation), which means continuing to work at a challenging task, making successful *and* unsuccessful attempts to complete the task. Children with Down syndrome tend to display poor task persistence; they often do not attempt the challenging tasks but instead, engage in other behavior, often socially interacting with the person who presented the task. This pattern illustrates the second factor, heightened social interest.

Social interest is a good thing, except when a child uses it to avoid engaging in learning opportunities. Plus, if a child has reduced interest in objects, it may affect how she responds when presented with opportunities to learn. Think about what happens in these problem-solving situations: after figuring out how to get the toy, such as by pulling the blanket in a means-end task, the child gets the toy. When manipulating a toy to explore it, the child gets to hear the sounds the toy makes and feel its texture. For children with Down syndrome, these object-related consequences often do not seem to be as rewarding as social consequences. Consequently, your child may be less likely to engage in skills that result in object-related consequences and will therefore miss opportunities to learn about her environment. We will show you how to use your child's heightened social interest to your advantage during intervention, rather than letting it hinder learning opportunities.

Academic Performance

Academic performance is also affected by executive functions such as problem solving. You may be thinking that mathematics is a good example of problem solving; if so, you are right. And if you also predicted that mathematics is an area of difficulty for children with Down syndrome, you would be right again. Differences begin in infancy when most young children with Down syndrome (unlike typically developing children) do not appear to discriminate between arrays of two and three items, an early measure of number skills. As counting develops, children with Down syndrome are challenged by counting each item just once (referred to as *one-to-one correspondence*). However, using manipulatives seems to help them with more sophisticated math skills such as addition and subtraction. Even children with Down syndrome who have memorized numerical facts tend to rely on manipulatives rather than using more abstract procedures to solve math problems.

Reading is another academic area in which children with Down syndrome show both strengths and weakness. Reading involves word recognition (being able to identify the word) and comprehension (knowing the meaning). Many children with Down syndrome learn to read, although ability varies and is usually delayed compared to chronological age.

Children with Down syndrome may actually have an advantage in learning to read *sight words,* something that may be related to strong visual processing. With sight word reading, children memorize the word as a whole unit, but every word must be specifically taught. To read words never seen before, however, requires decoding skills (sounding words out), and that relies on a phonological approach to reading. *Phonological* and *phonemic awareness* have to do with understanding the sounds of language and usually pose some difficulties for children with Down syndrome. Reading skills are also influenced by short-term memory and language development, highlighting how different areas of development interact. This is one reason we encourage you to implement the intervention programs for the different areas of development at the same time. For example, as you work on vocabulary, you will actually be helping your child develop skills that will support her reading.

Self-Care Skills

Independence is an essential goal for all children, even those who have significant challenges. One area of independence relates to learning to care for one's personal needs, referred to as self-care skills. By *self-care* we mean tasks related to personal hygiene and daily living. In early childhood, self-care skills include mealtime skills (eating and drinking) as well as dressing and toileting. As caregivers, we sometimes underestimate how much a young child can learn to do for herself. Keep in mind, the more a child can do for herself, the less reliant she will be on others, which in turn will help your child meet her full potential. Independence in self-care tasks is a huge milestone for all children and may provide a significant sense of what is referred to as *self-determination*—the extent to which a person has control over her own life.

Early mealtime skills include sucking on a breast or bottle, drinking from a straw and a cup, eating solid foods, and eventually eating independently with fingers and utensils. Eating requires that your child use a combination of tongue, lip, and jaw movements, all of which are controlled by oral facial muscles. Take a drink of water now or pretend to go through the actions. Think about all of the parts of the *oral cavity* (the parts of the mouth behind the teeth and gums within the hard and soft palate and below the tongue you use while taking a sip and swallowing). All of those movements require strength and movement of muscles; remember, these are called *oral motor skills.* For children with Down syndrome, typical differences in oral motor skills include tongue protrusion, atypical tongue movements, problems with lip closure, and poor jaw control, which all affect mealtime skills. Having a smaller oral cavity and low muscle tone also affects mealtime skills.

One concern for children with disabilities is eating a range of foods, flavors, textures, and consistencies. Too often, babies and children with disabilities do not eat a variety of different foods. This is referred to as *food selectivity*. Consuming a limited range of foods not only affects oral motor skill development but can also result in serious health problems. Teaching your child to eat a variety of foods will be easier to do when she is young and likely become more difficult the longer she continues to eat only a narrow range of foods.

Mealtime skills are also important to address because there is more going on when a child eats and drinks than just getting nourishment. In fact, all the movements and muscles that are involved in suckling on a nipple or chewing a crunchy cracker help to shape the oral cavity, which, in addition to the movement of the tongue, are essential for the development of speech sounds. To illustrate, try this: say, "Little Italy" a few times slowly. Notice how the parts of your mouth move to form each of the sounds. Well, the oral motor skills developed through feeding are the very same ones used for speech. So, the movements your child uses when eating and drinking are the same ones she will be using when developing speech.

In addition to developing oral motor skills and ensuring healthy eating, it is important to work on mealtime skills because they may be complicated by several factors associated with Down syndrome:

- Cardiac problems cause fatigue, which often results in decreased food and liquid consumption.
- Swallowing disorders can result in food or liquid entering the baby's windpipe.
- Thrusting the tongue forward can prevent the child from sucking and removing food from a spoon or fork or interfere with proper chewing.
- Jaw stability problems interfere with the child's ability to chew.
- Gastrointestinal problems can result from constipation or swallowing food that was not chewed.

Motor skills affect other self-care skills besides mealtime skills. Dressing and toileting both require fine motor skills that may make the tasks particularly difficult. In fact, the most delayed self-care skills in children with Down syndrome are those requiring fine motor movements. Dressing includes tying, pulling on and off pants and shirts, and fastening with zippers, buttons, and snaps. Children also need to learn hygiene skills such as tooth and hair brushing. Sometimes these basic self-care skills can remain obstacles for adolescents with Down syndrome.

Behavior That Interferes with Learning

There are some behaviors that enhance a child's learning: sitting attentively, looking at caregivers and instructional materials, and listening to instructions, among others. In contrast, other behaviors can interfere with learning; these range from poor attention to what we classically think of as problem or challenging behaviors such as having a tantrum.

For children with Down syndrome, some phenotypic characteristics may enhance learning. Characteristics such as being social and having a positive mood may mean children are likely to be motivated by interacting with parents or other caregivers and tend to have overall pleasant attitudes that can make instruction fun. But, as we discussed above, these same social behaviors may also interfere with learning. In fact, there seems to be a pattern—when faced with slightly difficult tasks (e.g., a learning task in a classroom, being asked to say words, etc.), children with Down syndrome have a tendency to show overly social behavior that distracts caregivers from the task. They also tend to have poor task persistence and perhaps use other behavior to get out of the task. Let's talk more about each of these factors.

Often children with Down syndrome engage in social behavior in situations when it might not be the most appropriate response. For example, when asked to imitate a word, a child may instead try to engage the adult in a game of making silly faces. Although it may not seem like a problem, overly social behavior can be disruptive to learning and likely begins at a very young age. Adults will likely respond with social interaction that also stops the task or instruction, which prevents the child from participating in learning opportunities and, as you will learn, increases the likelihood she will continue to respond that way when given instructions in the future.

Poor task persistence or mastery motivation can also have a negative impact on learning. As we discussed, children show task persistence when they look at the task and try different ways to complete it, maintaining their efforts for a reasonable period of time. Children with Down syndrome are not only more likely to take longer to begin or complete the task, but they also often engage in a variety of non-task-related behaviors and stay on task for shorter periods of time. Some of the non-task-related behavior is the social behavior we just described. They may also engage in problem behavior (e.g., pushing materials away or tantrums) or noncompliance (i.e., avoidance of or refusal to complete the task).

Jennifer Wishart's research clearly highlights this pattern of behavior and provides insight into the situations in which these behaviors are likely to occur. She found children with Down syndrome showed poor task persistence when faced with slightly difficult tasks as well as easy tasks. In an instructional situation, this means children may show these behaviors when you are teaching a new skill (difficult task) and even when you are providing assistance or prompts to make learning the new skill easier (easier task). The result is many missed learning opportunities.

Another behavior common in children with Down syndrome that interferes with learning is *repetitive behavior*. Repetitive behaviors are those that occur too frequently (i.e., over and over again), often with some rigidity or inflexibility. They range from stereotypical motor behavior such as twirling or rocking to more complex behaviors that you might think of as obsessive-compulsive-like such as checking things or hand washing. These behaviors can begin in young children and, unfortunately, often predict later problem behavior. One reason children may engage in repetitive behavior is because doing so results in pleasurable consequences that come from within the child (i.e., they do not require another person's involvement). For example, when a child repeatedly waves her fingers in front of her eyes, she gets to see an interesting visual display. One term used to describe these types of behaviors is *self-stimulatory*.

What Does Behavioral Phenotype Tell Us?

Now that you have information about the strengths and weaknesses in children with Down syndrome, what do you do with that information? We use behavioral phenotype to help us identify the following:

- skills to monitor—to be sure you can address difficulties (the same way you monitor your child's hearing and vision to correct any problems)
- skills that warrant intervention
- skills that are necessary to teach your child to then address areas of weakness—for example, teaching her to follow one-step instructions so that you can string them together to work on increasing memory skills
- skills to prevent further delay or deficit—for example, teaching your child to imitate speech sounds at an early age so she practices producing the sound correctly. If you do not do this, your child will likely begin to say the sound incorrectly and may do so for months or years before it is addressed. If this happens, you will spend extra time trying to correct the child's speech.
- strengths to use to tailor intervention, which may result in a more effective and efficient intervention. The interventions described in Book 2

will build on your child's relative strengths in social interest and visual processing. We do this by providing social attention when your child practices a skill (e.g., imitating your speech sounds) and even by creating social situations in which teaching can be embedded (such as teaching your child to make requests within social interactions). We also discuss using visuals to help your child learn new skills (e.g., showing your child a picture to help her remember what to do).

So, the Down syndrome behavioral phenotype helps us know *what* to intervene upon and even gives us ideas to tailor interventions to phenotypic strengths. Leaders in the field of Down syndrome such as Robert Hodapp, Deborah Fidler, Susan Hepburn, and Lynn Nadel have called for developing these types of interventions based on the cause (etiology) of a child's disability (etiology-based interventions). In this case, interventions are tailored for children with Down syndrome to specifically address phenotypic weaknesses and do so by building on strengths.

What behavioral phenotype does not tell us is *how* to intervene or teach those critical skills. We discuss how next.

HOW DO WE TEACH YOUNG CHILDREN WITH DOWN SYNDROME?

As soon as you learned your child had Down syndrome, you were likely thrust into a world of services and intervention options that you probably never knew existed. You have likely been told about a range of treatments, interventions, or educational approaches (terms that are used interchangeably throughout this manual). It is also likely that you have been referred to a number of doctors and other professionals. In this manual, you will find psychosocial, behavioral, and educational interventions, rather than biomedical approaches (such as medication).

Evidence-Based Intervention

In Chapter 1 we discussed interventions based on evidence from research. *Evidence-based interventions* are those that have been demonstrated to be effective in improving outcomes (e.g., social-communication, cognitive, academic, and motor skills as well as independence, self-care, and quality of life) through several research studies. The interventions described in this manual are evidence-based or have, at their foundation, evidence-based procedures.

The outcomes for your child—her quality of life, her access to the community, a job when she becomes an adult—are influenced by the interventions she receives. If an intervention has been shown to result in the outcomes you want for your child, then it is an intervention you want to pursue. If it has not, then there is the potential for the intervention to waste your time and your child's time, and even prevent your child from learning important skills.

When you know that there is research to support an intervention, you can

- spend your time and your child's time participating in interventions that are likely to result in the kinds of improvements and outcomes you desire,
- advocate for your child by presenting research articles to service providers and agency or school administrators so that your child can receive interventions that are likely to improve outcomes, and
- avoid interventions for which there is no evidence.

What Constitutes Evidence?

When you hear about an intervention, ask yourself this: *What evidence supports the use of this intervention with my child?* Is it enough that someone shared his or her family's story about how the intervention helped their child? Is it enough that a doctor described how he or she used a treatment with one or a handful of children? Is an article found on the Internet always considered evidence?

If you were unsure or answered "no" to these questions, you likely had concerns about whether these were truly evidence. These types of reports are considered *anecdotal* and are *not* considered evidence. Think of it this way: would you take a drug that was tested on only one or two people? Would you take a drug that your neighbor gave you because he or she said it worked? Or, would you expect that there would be extensive research on the effectiveness of the drug, including identifying side effects the drug may cause? Most of us would expect the latter when it comes to a drug, and many of us who are dedicated to evidence-based interventions expect the same type of scrutiny when it comes to educational, psychosocial, therapeutic and behavioral interventions.

We define evidence-based interventions as those that have been demonstrated to be effective through empirical research with multiple studies showing improvements in outcomes. *Empirical research* refers to studies or experiments conducted by trained researchers who base their findings on objective (i.e., nonbiased), observable, and measurable phenomena (e.g., behaviors, test scores). Empirical research studies are *experiments* that derive knowledge about the world based on actual experiences and facts, not just subjective theories, beliefs, or ideas that have not been tested. When researchers conduct experiments they

- measure and compare behavior (e.g., speech, reading, solving problems, etc.) before and after the intervention has been implemented to see if there was a change,
- carefully compare one intervention to another, and
- carefully control the interventions to be sure that any improvements they find are really caused by the intervention and not something else.

To illustrate, in one of the author's recent studies, Sara Bauer and Emily Jones (2015) examined an intervention to improve requesting (i.e., when a child asks for things she would like) and vocal imitation (imitating sounds) in infants with Down syndrome. We defined vocal imitation as a baby repeating, exactly, the sounds her caregiver made (e.g., "ma," buh," "d," etc.). We measured vocal imitation every time we asked the baby to imitate a sound, and did so before, during, and after intervention (described shortly). We also measured how well other people understood each baby's sounds before and after intervention.

We identified a few sounds each of the babies did *not* imitate (e.g., saying, "ma" or "buh") when we asked them to imitate (e.g., the baby's caregiver said, "Say, 'buh'" without any intervention). Then we began intervention addressing one sound at a time for each baby. The intervention involved many opportunities to imitate and strategies for getting the baby to make certain sounds (e.g., gently touching the baby's lips), and we responded with smiles, praise, and tickles after the baby imitated a sound. We compared how the baby imitated each sound before intervention began and during intervention. If the intervention truly improved vocal imitation, a baby's imitation would improve when the intervention was implemented on that particular sound. That was exactly what happened. When the intervention was implemented with each sound, each baby imitated that sound. Also, other people were better able to identify many of the sounds after intervention than they were before intervention. So, we were able to *empirically* demonstrate that the intervention was effective in developing speech sounds and in developing them in a way that others understood them.

At this point, you are probably recalling doing experiments in science courses in high school or college, and you are thinking along the right lines. Conducting systematic experiments is exactly what researchers do to demonstrate the effectiveness of an intervention.

Research studies are published in professional journals that have a peer review process. **Peer review** means a group of experts evaluate the quality of each study. This means the study is examined by other experts as an extra check to be sure it meets high standards of quality before it is published for the rest of the world to see. Some journals that use a peer review process and publish intervention studies related to Down syndrome include the following:

- *American Journal of Intellectual and Developmental Disabilities* (previous titles include *American Journal on Mental Retardation* and *American Journal on Mental Deficiency*)
- *Applied Research in Mental Retardation* (incorporated into *Research in Developmental Disabilities*)
- *Augmentative and Alternative Communication*
- *Behavioral Interventions*
- *Behavior Modification*
- *Down Syndrome Research and Practice*
- *Education and Training in Developmental Disabilities* (previously titled *Education and Training in Autism and Developmental Disabilities*)
- *Journal of Applied Behavior Analysis*
- *Journal of Developmental and Physical Disabilities*
- *Journal of Positive Behavior Interventions*
- *Research in Developmental Disabilities*

The studies published in these journals are in contrast to reports published by the authors themselves in venues where a peer review process is not likely done (e.g., newsletters, magazines, websites, etc.). You can find research articles by visiting your public library or a local college or university library and searching their databases. For example, if you wanted to know about speech intervention for children with Down syndrome, you might type those words into the database.

The Internet is a great place for information, but it can be a bit problematic, as anything can be placed on a website, and it does not mean that it is accurate. Evidence-based interventions from peer-reviewed journal articles are often described on websites and even in popular magazines. Most of the time, these descriptions will include the name of the journal and the authors, so you can find the original article in the peer-reviewed journal. Sometimes there will be a list of references at the end of the article. But, be careful, because sometimes what looks like research is not. Sometimes references are just to other websites or magazine articles. Just start clicking on links—if you keep clicking and realize that none of the links take you to any research study or journal website, what you are reading about is probably not research. When references are to an actual journal article, you will likely be taken to a copy of the article or to the journal website where the article was published. Then you can read it to see if it is truly an empirical study.

To help you search specifically for journal publications on the Internet, use a search engine such as Google Scholar that focuses on journal publications. Once you find an article you want to read, you will have to access that article. Some journals have free access through the Internet. Others require a payment, or you can often access them through your local library by requesting an interlibrary loan (just ask!).

Advanced Information ➞ Experimental Designs

To determine if a particular intervention does, in fact, enhance performance, experiments are conducted. There are two types of experiments. **Group designs** test an intervention on one or more groups of individuals; **single subject designs** test an intervention on one person at a time. There are several different types of studies for each type of design.

Group Designs. Sometimes researchers take a group of individuals, determine how they perform, provide an intervention, and examine how they perform again after the intervention. Then they compare performance before and after the intervention. This is a pre-post design and can suggest that an intervention might be effective. The biggest concern with this design is that the group of individuals might have improved simply because of the passage of time or some other event (e.g., a classroom of students improved their reading performance not because of the research program being studied, but because the teacher also started doing small group review sessions). These other factors that could explain why the group improved pre- to post-intervention are referred to as *confounding variables*. This makes it difficult to conclude that an intervention was truly effective with a pre-post design.

The gold standard group design to demonstrate the effectiveness of an intervention is referred to as a **randomized controlled trial**. Children who are similar in many ways (e.g., all have a specific disability, are the same age, or share a similar set of skills) are randomly assigned either to the group that receives the intervention (the experimental group) or to the group that does not receive the intervention or receives another intervention (the control group). The overall performance of the two groups is then compared. The only thing that differs between the two groups is the presence of the intervention being tested. If the experimental group performs better following the intervention, this suggests that the intervention caused the improvements in performance. If the two groups perform similarly following the intervention, then any changes in performance could not be attributed to the intervention.

(continued)

Now, it is often very difficult for researchers to randomly assign participants to groups, because many logistical and ethical issues may arise. For example, in an intervention study in which the children are randomly assigned to groups, half of the children would not get the intervention (as they would be assigned to the no intervention group). Sometimes groups of children are not randomly assigned, but already exist, such as two different classrooms or schools. Then one classroom or school receives the intervention (experimental group) and the other does not (control group). If the experimental group performs better, this suggests the intervention improved performance. However, if there was no difference between the two groups, the intervention was likely not effective. The problem with this design is that existing groups could be different in other ways (remember, these are *confounding* variables) that affect how they perform and respond to the intervention. Random assignment minimizes the likelihood that groups will differ in any other relevant ways. That is why random assignment is a defining part of rigorous experimental group designs.

Single Subject Designs. In single subject designs, the performance of one or a small number of individuals is measured before, during, and after intervention. The performance measured before the intervention is referred to as **baseline** performance. Often, this entails observing the child and documenting whether a specific behavior occurred and, if it did, how often. Then, an intervention is implemented. The researchers continue to measure the child's performance while the intervention is being conducted and compare it to the child's performance prior to the intervention (i.e., during baseline). The child's performance is illustrated on a graph and the data points are examined to look for differences between baseline and intervention performance. To demonstrate that the findings can be generalized (i.e., are likely to occur in others who receive the same intervention), the procedures are replicated with a few more children.

Just comparing baseline to intervention performance is not enough to clearly demonstrate that it was the intervention, and nothing else, that resulted in improvement in the child's performance. It is just like with the pre-post group design described previously; several other things could have happened at the same time. For example, the child may have not

(continued)

been feeling well during baseline and then recovered during intervention, or another intervention may have been implemented at the same time as the one being studied. Researchers use several specific single subject designs in order to control for these sorts of confounding variables. Here are a few common experimental designs that you will likely encounter as you read single subject design studies:

In a *reversal design*, the sequence of baseline and intervention is repeated. This means that following baseline, researchers introduce the intervention and then withdraw the intervention; they then repeat baseline and then repeat the intervention again. This provides experimental control, because it would be highly unlikely that one or more confounding variables would occur at the exact time that the intervention was implemented each time the intervention was introduced.

In an *alternating treatments design*, two different interventions are compared by rapidly alternating them. This means the researcher provides one intervention during one session or day and then provides the other intervention the next session or day. The researchers keep alternating the interventions that way. If one intervention works better than the other, then, over time, the child's performance will improve in the one intervention and always be lower in the second intervention.

In a *multiple baseline design*, three or more individuals, behaviors, or settings are identified. Baseline performance is examined for all three. Then, the intervention is implemented with one individual, behavior, or setting at a time, while the second and third individuals, behaviors, or settings do not receive intervention (i.e., they stay on baseline). When performance improves for the first individual, behavior, or setting, then intervention begins for the second, while the third continues on baseline, and so on. If the intervention (and not some other variable) is causing improvements in performance, then performance will improve only when the intervention is implemented (and not during the baselines for the three individuals, behaviors, or settings). If performance changes are *not* due to the intervention, but rather to some other variable or variables (such as child maturation or another intervention), then performance will change during the baseline conditions before intervention begins.

Knowing what the research says will be helpful as you advocate for your child, but it can be a daunting task. So, let's discuss how to evaluate different interventions and the research.

. . . .

Making Sense of All the Different Interventions

At this point you have probably asked your pediatrician and other doctors about different interventions. You have probably searched the Internet and may even have participated in parent groups or received other services and been told about even more interventions. Asking and networking are great first steps in learning about the resources that are out there for you and your child. Doing so will also help you develop a network of support for your family. But this can leave you overwhelmed with many options from which to choose.

Some families will decide to try the intervention that is popular, endorsed with anecdotes from other parents, or recommended by "experts" or "authority figures." Some families will "try everything," with the hope that one of the interventions will work. Families will often be told, "You'll never know until you try it" or "Not everything works for every child." But keep these points in mind:

- If you try everything, you and your child will spend a little bit of time participating in many interventions. It might not be enough time for any one of the interventions to be effective. Thus, your child may not receive the right amount of intervention for it to have its intended impact.
- If you try everything, you and your child may participate in interventions that actually conflict with and counteract each other. This may prevent your child from benefiting from either intervention, or worse, negatively affect your child's progress. Thus, implementing one intervention may result in "undoing" positive changes from another intervention.

Instead, we recommend you look at the research studies of an intervention you are considering for your child. The research studies that support evidence-based interventions have important characteristics: an experimental design, clearly described intervention procedures, and observable measures of behavior (which means behaviors were identified and then closely monitored to see if the intervention caused them to change). These are not stories about an intervention or stories from one or a handful of people who "think" the intervention was effective. Instead, research studies clearly describe each step of the intervention and provide evidence for how the intervention worked.

When considering an intervention, ask yourself these questions:

- Who conducted the research to determine whether it is effective?

- How did they determine whether the intervention worked?
  - ➤ Did they observe the child before and after the intervention?
  - ➤ Did they observe and compare the performance of a group of children who received the intervention to those who did not?
  - ➤ Was the intervention compared to another intervention?
- Did studies show improvements in a behavior that you are concerned about for your child?
- Where did the researchers describe their findings?

What Does the Research Say about Intervention for Children with Down Syndrome?

We have made a point about the importance of having research to support an intervention. And we even suggested that you look for that research. But reading through all the research literature can be a daunting task. We do it every day, but that is our job! One way researchers help people understand what individual research studies say about an intervention is that they put all the studies together, carefully analyze them, and provide a summary of whether (and the extent to which) the individual studies suggest an intervention is effective. These are referred to as comprehensive or systematic reviews and meta-analyses. Such reviews help parents and professionals identify and access interventions that have research to support their effectiveness.

In 2006, the New York State Department of Health (NYSDOH) systematically reviewed research literature on early intervention services for children with Down syndrome. As a result, they published the *Clinical Practice Guideline for Down Syndrome: Assessment and Intervention for Young Children (Age 0–3 Years)*. This is a review of all the intervention literature available at the time for young children with Down syndrome. A panel of experts, including professionals and researchers in the field of early intervention, clinicians, and educators, along with parents of children with Down syndrome, reviewed the research and provided recommendations for assessment and interventions for infants and young children (birth to three years) specifically with Down syndrome.

What Interventions for Children with Down Syndrome Are Effective?

The *NYSDOH Clinical Practice Guideline for Down Syndrome* concluded that a number of interventions lack an evidence base, because no scientific studies were found to provide evidence that these interventions improved or advanced skills in infants and children with Down syndrome. Some of these therapies include music therapy, art therapy, therapeutic horseback riding (hippotherapy), and conductive education (training to develop alternate neural pathways to create more functional motor patterns).

Across domains of development, the *NYSDOH Clinical Practice Guideline for Down Syndrome* repeatedly recommended intervention involving techniques from **applied behavior analysis (ABA).** However, the authors did not use the term applied behavior analysis within the guidelines. Rather, they used terms such as *operant conditioning techniques, principles of learning theory,* and *behavior modification.* All these terms are related and, as discussed in Chapter 1, have to do with a science devoted to determining the environmental variables that explain and improve behavior. Remember, when we described applied behavior analysis in Chapter 1, we said that behavior analytic strategies focus on changing what comes before a desired behavior and what follows that behavior to increase the likelihood that behavior occurs again.

The NYSDOH guideline recommended that intervention include behavior analytic strategies such as reinforcement, especially to teach new skills and facilitate generalization. **Reinforcement** occurs when something that happens after a behavior causes that behavior to increase in the future. Reinforcers include such things as the child being given stickers, praise, or friendly interactions or access to fun activities (getting to bounce on a trampoline or read a book with Dad). For example, when Susie says "Hello" to her teacher, her teacher could say "Hello" back and give Susie a smile and a high five. On subsequent mornings, if Susie continues to say "Hello," then reinforcement has occurred; Susie's teacher said "Hello" and gave Susie a smile and high five and Susie's behavior (saying "Hello") increased.

An important component of intervention is breaking skills into smaller, measurable behaviors that are targeted for change. We refer to these as **targets**. Intervention also involves providing multiple learning opportunities and continuously monitoring progress, each of which will be described in more detail in Chapter 3 in this book, where you will learn all about behavior analytic strategies.

The conclusions from the 2006 *NYSDOH Clinical Practice Guideline* were based on a very small number of studies. Fourteen studies were judged rigorous enough to provide evidence to support applied behavior analysis with children with Down syndrome in the areas of cognitive and communication/language development. As a result, the recommendation for applied behavior analysis was based on limited evidence. However, there are additional studies not included (for various reasons) in the NYSDOH guideline that include children with Down syndrome that add to the evidence base supporting a behavior analytic approach to intervention.

What Else Do We Know about Applied Behavior Analysis for Children with Down Syndrome?

The additional studies from the time period up to the 2006 review include studies in which all the children who participated had Down syndrome as well as many studies of heterogeneous groups of participants (perhaps with only one or a few children with Down syndrome). The studies that include only participants with Down syndrome clearly demonstrated the effectiveness of behavior analytic interventions with this group of children. Other studies that were not included in the 2006 *NYSDOH Clinical Practice Guideline for Down Syndrome* involved children older than three years (the age range for the 2006 review was birth to three years only) and adults with Down syndrome. These studies showed positive effects for older children and adults with Down syndrome.

At the end of this chapter, we have listed a number of studies that demonstrate the effectiveness of behavior analytic interventions with individuals with Down syndrome. We are sure this does not include every study, but it illustrates there are many empirical studies across areas of development.

Recently, one of us (Neil & Jones, 2016) completed a review of the research on interventions to address communication skills in children with Down syndrome. We did not limit our search to behavior analytic interventions; rather, we looked for any type of psychosocial intervention. We only identified thirty-seven studies in which all of the participants in the study had Down syndrome. A total of 225 individuals with Down syndrome participated in the thirty-seven studies. The majority of the studies used behavior analytic interventions, and when the results were combined and subjected to statistical tests, behavior analytic intervention was found to result in significant improvements in communication skills for individuals with Down syndrome.

Comprehensive Curricula Addressing Multiple Areas of Development

The behavior analytic research described so far focused on select procedures and interventions for specific behaviors (e.g., communication, academic skills) but did not represent comprehensive interventions designed to address the range of needs of children with Down syndrome—what we are doing in this book. The first comprehensive intervention with empirical evidence was published in 1978— yes, 1978; it is not a typo. In 1978 Marci Hanson and Robert H. Schwarz published "Results of a Longitudinal Intervention Program for Down's Syndrome Infants and Their Families." Hanson then published her curriculum in 1987. The behavior analytic intervention involved breaking skills into small parts, presenting multiple opportunities, and using instructions, prompting, and reinforcement. For example, to teach a child to reach for an object, Hanson suggested that caregivers provide multiple opportunities and prompt the child by placing one hand on the infant's hand and moving it toward the object being reached for. Once reaching occurred, caregivers provided praise. The intervention was designed to be implemented by parents at home with their infants and toddlers.

In the 1978 study, Hanson and Schwarz followed twelve infants with Down syndrome who participated in this intervention. Children started before they turned six months of age and remained in intervention for fifteen to thirty months. A parent advisor visited weekly or biweekly to help evaluate the child's performance, identify goals, and write interventions for the parent to follow daily with his or her child. Parents taught four to five skills each week, providing ten opportunities for each skill per day. Children reached developmental milestones (including feeding, gross motor, and language) well ahead of the "norms" that were available for children with Down syndrome at the time. Some language goals were achieved at the same time we would expect typically developing children to do so. In a follow-up study, Hanson (2003) continued to find overall positive effects.

There are a few other early intervention curricula like Hanson's that are specifically for children with Down syndrome and include behavior analytic strategies for addressing a range of skills (e.g., Dmitriev, 2001). It should be noted however, that not all have research evaluating their effects.

Research about Behavior Analytic Interventions for Young Children with Down Syndrome

Although the NYSDOH Clinical Practice Guideline for Down Syndrome recommendations were published in 2006, leading researchers in the field of Down syndrome are still calling for empirically demonstrated, behavior analytic interventions (Buckley, 2008). They are also calling for interventions that specifically integrate what we know about the Down syndrome behavioral phenotype to address weaknesses and build on strengths (e.g., Fidler, Most, & Philofsky, 2008; Fidler & Nadel, 2007; Hodapp & Fidler, 1999).

There has been a growing body of research since 2006 examining behavior analytic interventions specifically for young children with Down syndrome that address phenotypic weaknesses. Recently, researchers have begun looking very carefully at interventions to address the weakness in requesting (e.g., Bauer & Jones, 2015; Feeley, Jones, Blackburn, & Bauer, 2011; Jones, Feeley & Blackburn, 2010; Fey, Warren, Brady, Finestock, Brendin-Oja, & Fairchild et al., 2006; Yoder & Warren, 2002). In our own ongoing clinical work and research, understanding behavioral phenotype has helped us tailor these interventions. For example, we found that intervention seems to work better when complex requesting skills are taught in smaller target steps (e.g., first teaching a baby to look, then adding a gesture or a sound). We continue to research the best ways to provide instruction for children with Down syndrome. We have learned, however, that it is particularly important to follow these guidelines:

- Use specific prompts to help children engage in skills you want to teach and then systematically fade those prompts until the child performs independently.
- Carefully choose reinforcement procedures that involve social attention, which many children with Down syndrome enjoy, increasing motivation and thus, learning.
- Provide multiple repeated opportunities, often five to ten in a row, with very little time between opportunities to practice each skill. This results in rapid skill acquisition. Not only does number of opportunities seem important, but in recent work we have found that the spacing between opportunities is critical for skill acquisition. In fact, only a small number of seconds between opportunities results in better performance. So, it is quite fast-paced instruction.

WHERE DO WE TEACH?

In Chapter 1 we introduced two key components of our approach: (1) an understanding of behavioral phenotype and (2) applied behavior analysis. A third, and critical, component is access to environments shared by typical peers. Now, the field has many names for this, including *least restrictive environment*, *mainstreaming*, and *inclusion*. We prefer the term **inclusion**, which means children with disabilities participate in the same community activities and educational opportunities they would have if they did not have a disability. For schools, this means children with disabilities attend the same school in the same class as they would have if they had not had a disability. Now, this does not necessarily mean that *all* instruction is provided in *all* subject areas in that setting *all* day. Rather, the child receives supports and services to meet her individual needs.

Sometimes parents and other caregivers with whom we work think behavior analytic intervention cannot be provided within inclusive environments. This belief seems to be most common in communities where specialized services are provided outside of community schools (i.e., in specialized schools). But using behavior analytic interventions is about *how* we teach, not *where* we teach. Thus, behavior analytic interventions can certainly be developed and implemented within community schools.

Fortunately, in the United States, federal legislation supports children with disabilities being educated alongside their typical peers. The Individuals with Disabilities Education Act (IDEA) includes a provision that children with disabilities be educated in the *least restrictive environment* (LRE). That means children should be educated alongside children without disabilities to the maximum extent possible.

In early childhood, LRE means homes, day care centers, and preschools. Much of the research with babies and very young children with Down syndrome that we have discussed was done in families' homes with the parents providing intervention (e.g., Bidder, Bryant, & Gray, 1975; Clunies-Ross, 1979; Hanson & Schwartz, 1978). Also, the *NYSDOH Clinical Practice Guideline for Down Syndrome* (2006) recommended teaching opportunities with peers to help children with Down syndrome develop cognitive, social-communication, and other skills.

Just as there is evidence to support behavior analytic interventions with children with Down syndrome, there is research to support educating children with Down syndrome alongside their typical peers. Teaching school-aged children with Down syndrome in an inclusive setting results in more positive outcomes than education in a separate special education class setting (Buckley, Bird, Sacks, & Archer, 2006; Buckley, Bird, & Sacks, 2006). It also results in vast gains in literacy and expressive language (a prime area of weakness in children with Down syndrome) and can perhaps even alter the pattern of cognitive and social-communication weaknesses we have described in this chapter.

Often individualized goals and one-to-one support from a professional experienced in teaching children with Down syndrome are needed. The evidence presented in the research indicates that, if these resources are available, children with Down syndrome will flourish academically in an inclusive setting, more so than in a nonintegrated setting (Buckley, Bird, Sacks, & Archer, 2006; Buckley, Bird, & Sacks, 2006; Turner, Alborz, & Gayle, 2008; Couzens, Haynes, & Cuskelly, 2012; de Graaf, van Hove, & Haveman, 2012).

Our Model

We have combined our clinical work with our research and that of others over the past several decades to identify the *what, how,* and *where* of intervention for young children with Down syndrome. The result is

- a curriculum that focuses on areas identified as weaknesses associated with the Down syndrome behavioral phenotype and
- a behavior analytic approach to intervention consistent with empirical evidence building on phenotypic strengths that
- involves placement of children with Down syndrome alongside typically developing peers.

We continue to examine the what, how, and where of intervention for young children with Down syndrome through ongoing research and clinical work at the Developmental Disabilities Lab at Queens College, City University of New York, and the Center for Community Inclusion at Long Island University (LIU Post).

Applied Behavior Analysis Research with Individuals with Down Syndrome

Listed below are many studies that demonstrate the effectiveness of behavior analytic interventions with individuals with Down syndrome. We organized this list by the areas of development we discussed in this chapter. We hope you can see that there are numerous studies demonstrating the effectiveness of applied behavior analysis with children with Down syndrome (and we are pretty sure there are more).

Studies That Addressed Multiple Areas of Development

Bidder, R. T., Bryant, G., & Gray, O. P. (1975). Benefits to Down's syndrome children through training their mothers. *Archives of Disease in Childhood, 50,* 383–386.

Clunies-Ross, G. G. (1979). Accelerating the development of Down's syndrome infants and young children. *The Journal of Special Education, 13* (2), 169–177.

Hanson, M. J. (2003). Twenty-five years after early intervention: A follow-up of children with Down syndrome and their families. *Infants and Young Children, 16* (4), 354–365.

Hanson, M. J., & Schwarz, R. H. (1978). Results of a longitudinal intervention program for Down's syndrome infants and their families. *Education and Training of the Mentally Retarded, 13* (4), 403–407.

Hayden, A. H., & Dmitriev, V. (1975). The multidisciplinary preschool program for Down's syndrome children at the University of Washington Model Preschool Center. In B. Z. Friedlander, G. M. Sterritt, & G. E. Kirk (Eds.). *Exceptional Infant: Assessment & Intervention* (Vol. 3) (pp. 193–221). New York: Brunner/Mazel.

Lafasakis, M., & Sturmey, P. (2007). Training parent implementation of discrete-trial teaching: Effects on generalization of parent teaching and child correct responding. *Journal of Applied Behavior Analysis, 40* (4), 685–689. doi: 10.1901/ jaba.2007.685–689.

Rynders, J., Abery, B. H., Spiker, D., Olive, M. L., Sheran, C. P., & Zajac, R. J. (1997). Improving educational programming for individuals with Down syndrome: Engaging the fuller competence. *Down Syndrome Quarterly, 2,* 1–11.

Sanz Aparicio, M. T. (1988). Effect of observational training of parents in the early stimulation of trisomy-21 babies. *Early Child Development and Care, 41,* 89–101.

Sanz Aparicio, M.T. (1989). Modeling and early language acquisitions in Down syndrome. *Early Child Development and Care, 44,* 51–59.

Sanz, M. T. (1996). A comparison of vicarious and written training techniques applied to early stimulation by parents of their Down syndrome babies. *Early Child Development and Care, 126,* 111–119.

Sanz, M. T., & Menéndez, F. J. (1993). Early acquisitions of trisomic-21 and social reinforcement. *Early Child Development and Care, 91,* 17–23.

Sanz, M. T., & Menéndez, F. J. (1995). A study of the effect of age of onset of treatment on the observed development of Down's syndrome babies. *Early Child Development and Care, 118,* 93–101.

Sanz Aparicio, M. T. (2004). Results from an experimental study about reinforcements employed in early training. *Early Child Development and Care, 174* (2), 193–198. doi: 10.1080/0300443032000153525.

Schepis, M. M., Reid, D. H., Ownbey, J., & Parsons, M. B. (2001). Training support staff to embed teaching within natural routines of young children with disabilities in an inclusive preschool. *Journal of Applied Behavior Analysis, 34* (3), 313–327.

Motor Development

Sanz Aparicio, M. T., & Menéndez Balana, F. J. (1992). Vicarious learning of parents and early motor acquisition of Down syndrome. *Early Child Development and Care, 83,* 27–31.

Sanz Aparicio, M. T., & Menéndez Balana, J. (2003). Early learning in psychomotor training of Down's syndrome. *Early Child Development and Care, 173* (2–3), 317–321. doi: 10.1080/0300443031000071851.

Sanz Aparicio, M. T., & Menéndez Balana, J. (2009). A study of early fine motor intervention in Down's syndrome children. *Early Child Development and Care, 179* (5), 631–636. doi: 10.1080/03004430701453754.

Social-Communication Development

Bauer, S., & Jones, E. A. (2014). A behavior analytic approach to exploratory motor (EM) behavior: How can caregivers teach EM behavior to infants with Down syndrome? *Infants and Young Children, 27* (2), 161–172. Doi: 10.1097/IYC.0000000000000004.

Bauer, S., & Jones, E. A. (2015). Requesting and verbal imitation intervention for infants with Down syndrome: Generalization, intelligibility, and problem solving. *Journal of Developmental and Physical Disabilities, 27,* 37–66. doi 10.1007/s10882-014-9400-6.

Bauer, S., Jones, E. A., & Feeley, K. M. (2014). Teaching responses to questions to young children with Down syndrome. *Behavioral Interventions, 29,* 36–49. Doi: 10.1002/bin.1368.

Bidder, R. T., Bryant, G., & Gray, O. P. (1975). Benefits to Down's syndrome children through training their mothers. *Archives of Disease in Childhood, 50,* 383–386.

Binger, C., & Light, J. (2007). The effects of aided AAC modeling on the expression of multi-symbol messages by preschoolers who use AAC. *Augmentative and Alternative Communication, 23* (1), 30–43. doi: 10.1080/07434610600807470.

Brinton, B., & Fujiki, M. (1996). Responses to requests for clarification by older and young adults with mental retardation. *Research in Developmental Disabilities, 17* (5), 335–347.

Chambers, M., & Rehfeldt, R. A. (2003). Assessing the acquisition and generalization of two mand forms with adults with severe developmental disabilities. *Research in Developmental Disabilities, 24,* 265–280. doi:10.1016/S0891-4222(03)00042-8.

Contrucci-Kuhn, S. A., Lerman, D. C., Vorndran, C. M., & Addison, L. (2006). Analysis of factors that affect responding in a two-response chain in children with developmental disabilities. *Journal of Applied Behavior Analysis, 39,* 263–280.

Cottrell, A. W., Montague, J., Farb, J., & Throne, J. M. (1980). An operant procedure for improving vocabulary definition performances in developmentally delayed children. *Journal of Speech and Hearing Disorders, 45* (1), 90–102.

Dalton, A. J., Rubino, C. A., & Hislop, M. W. (1973). Some effects of token rewards on school achievement of children with Down's syndrome. *Journal of Applied Behavior Analysis, 6* (2), 251–259.

Drash, P. W., Raver, S. A., Murrin, M. R., & Tudor, R. M. (1989). Three procedures for increasing vocal response to therapist prompt in infants and children with Down syndrome. *American Journal on Mental Retardation, 94* (1), 64–73.

Duker, P. C. & Michielsen, H. M. (1983). Cross-setting generalization of manual signs to verbal instructions with severely retarded children. *Applied Research in Mental Retardation, 4,* 29–40.

Duker, P. C., & Moonen, X. M. (1985). A program to increase manual signs with severely/profoundly mentally retarded students in natural environments. *Applied Research in Mental Retardation, 6,* 147–158.

Duker, P. C., & Moonen, X. M. (1986). The effect of two procedures on spontaneous signing with Down's syndrome children. *Journal of Mental Deficiency Research, 30,* 355–364.

Duker, P. C., & Morsink, H. (1984). Acquisition and cross-setting generalization of manual signs with severely retarded individuals. *Journal of Applied Behavior Analysis, 17* (1), 93–103.

Feeley, K. M., & Jones, E. A. (2008). Teaching spontaneous responses to a young child with Down syndrome. *Down Syndrome Research and Practice, 12,* 148–152.

Feeley, K. M., Jones, E. A., Blackburn, C., & Bauer, S. (2011). Advancing imitation and requesting skills in toddlers with Down syndrome. *Research in Developmental Disabilities, 32,* 2415–2430. doi: 10.1016/j.ridd.2011.07.018.

Fey, M. E., Warren, S. F., Brady, N., Finestack, L. H., Bredin-Oja, S. L., Fairchild, M., Sokol, S., & Yoder, P. J. (2006). Early effects of responsivity education/ prelinguistic milieu teaching for children with developmental delays and their parents. *Journal of Speech, Language, and Hearing Research, 49,* 526–547.

Goldstein, H., English, K., Shafer, K., & Kaczmarek, L. (1997). Interaction among preschoolers with and without disabilities: Effects of across-the-day peer intervention. *Journal of Speech, Language, and Hearing Research, 40* (1), 33–48.

Goodman, J., & Remington, B. (1993). Acquisition of expressive signing: Comparison reinforcement strategies. *Augmentative and Alternative Communication, 9,* 26-35.

Guitierrez, A., Vollmer, T. R., & Samaha, A. L. (2010). Developing and assessing stimulus control based on establishing operations during mand training using representative objects. *Behavioral Interventions, 25* (2), 169-182. doi:10.1002/ bin.302.

Gunn, P., Berry, P., & Andrews, R. (1979). Vocalization and looking behaviour of Down's syndrome infants. *British Journal of Psychology, 70,* 259–263.

Halle, J. W., & Holt, B. (1991). Assessing stimulus control in natural settings: An analysis of stimuli that acquire control during training. *Journal of Applied Behavior Analysis, 24* (3), 579–589.

Halle, J. W., Baer, D. M., & Spradlin, J. E. (1981). Teachers' generalized use of delay as a stimulus control procedure to increase language use in handicapped children. *Journal of Applied Behavior Analysis, 14* (4), 389–409.

Hanson, M. J., & Hanline, M. F. (1985). An analysis of response-contingent learning experiences for young children. *Journal of the Association for Persons with Severe Handicaps, 10* (1), 31–40.

Haring, T. G., Rogers, B., Lee, M., Breen, C., & Gaylord-Ross, R. (1986). Teaching social language to moderately handicapped students. *Journal of Applied Behavior Analysis, 19* (2), 159–171.

Heller, K. W., Allgood, M. H., Ware, S., Arnold, S. E., & Castelle, M. D. (1996). Initiating requests during community-based vocational training by students with mental retardation and sensory impairments. *Research in Developmental Disabilities, 17* (3), 173–184.

Hemmeter, M. L., Ault, M. J., Collins, B. C., & Meyer, S. (1996). The effects of teacher-implemented language instruction within free time activities. *Education and Training in Mental Retardation and Developmental Disabilities, 31* (3), 203– 212.

Hetzroni, O. E., & Roth, T. (2003). Effects of a positive support approach to enhance communicative behaviors of children with mental retardation who have challenging behaviors. *Education and Training in Developmental Disabilities, 38* (1), 95–105.

Hewitt, L. E., Hinkle, A. S., & Miccio, A. W. (2005). Intervention to improve expressive grammar for adults with Down syndrome. *Communication Disorders Quarterly, 26* (3), 144–155.

Holdgrafer, G. (1980). Facilitating syntax acquisition. *Psychological Reports, 46,* 498.

Hunt, P., Alwell, M., Goetz, L., & Sailor, W. (1990). Generalized effects of conversation skill training. *Journal of the Association for Persons with Severe Handicaps, 15,* 250–260.

Iacono, T. A., & Duncum, J. E. (1995). Comparison of sign alone and in combination with an electronic communication device in early language intervention: Case study. *Augmentative and Alternative Communication, 11,* 249–259.

Jones, E. A., Feeley, K. M., & Blackburn, C. (2010). A preliminary study of intervention addressing early developing requesting behaviours in young infants with Down syndrome. *Down Syndrome Research and Practice.* Advance online publication.

Kouri, T. A. (1988). Effects of simultaneous communication in a child-directed treatment approach with preschoolers with severe disabilities. *Augmentative and Alternative Communication, 4* (4), 222–232.

Kroeger, K. A., & Nelson III, W. M. (2006). A language programme to increase the verbal production of a child dually diagnosed with Down syndrome and autism. *Journal of Intellectual Disability Research, 50* (2), 101–108. doi: 10.1111/j.1365–2788.2005.00734.x.

Lane, S. D., & Critchfield, T. S. (1998). Classification of vowels and consonants by individuals with moderate mental retardation: Development of arbitrary relations via match-to-sample training with compound stimuli. *Journal of Applied Behavior Analysis, 31* (1), 21–41.

LeBlanc, L. A., Geiger, K. B., Sautter, R. A., & Sidener, T. M. (2007). Using the Natural Language Paradigm (NLP) to increase vocalizations of older adults with cognitive impairments. *Research in Developmental Disabilities, 28,* 437–444. doi:10.1016/j.ridd.2006.06.004.

Luciano, C., Barnes-Holmes, Y., & Barnes-Holmes, D. (2002). Establishing reports of saying and doing and discriminations of say-do relations. *Research in Developmental Disabilities, 23,* 406–421.

Luciano-Soriano, M. C., Molina-Cobos, F. J, & Gómez-Becerra, I. (2000). Say-do-report training to change chronic behaviors in mentally retarded subjects. *Research in Developmental Disabilities, 21,* 355–366.

MacCubrey, J. (1971). Verbal operant conditioning with young institutionalized Down's syndrome children. *American Journal of Mental Deficiency, 75* (6), 696–701.

McBride, B. J., & Schwartz, I. S. (2003). Effects of teaching early interventionists to use discrete trials during ongoing classroom activities. *Topics in Early Childhood Special Education, 23* (1), 5–17.

McDonnell, A. P. (1996). The acquisition, transfer, and generalization of requests by young children with severe disabilities. *Education and Training Mental Retardation and Developmental Disabilities, 31* (3), 213–233.

Martella, R., Marchand-Martella, N., Young, R., & MacFarlane, C. (1995). Determining the collateral effects of peer tutor training on a student with severe disabilities. *Behavior Modification, 19,* 170–191. doi: 10.1177/01454455950192002.

Mirenda, P., & Dattilo, J. (1987). Instructional techniques in alternative communication for students with severe intellectual handicaps. *Augmentative and Alternative Communication, 3* (3), 143–152.

Morgan, R. L., & Salzberg, C. L. (1992). Effects of video-assisted training on employment-related social skills of adults with severe mental retardation. *Journal of Applied Behavior Analysis, 25* (2), 365–383.

Neil, N., & Jones, E. A. (2015). Studying treatment intensity: Lessons learned from two preliminary studies. *Journal of Behavioral Education [Special issue: Treatment intensity], 24* (1), 51–73. doi 10.1007/s10864-014-9208-6.

Olenick, D. L., & Pear, J. J. (1980). Differential reinforcement of correct responses to probes and prompts in picture-name training with severely retarded children. *Journal of Applied Behavior Analysis, 13* (1), 77–89.

Osguthorpe, R. T., & Chang, L. L. (1988). The effects of computerized symbol processor instruction on the communication skills of nonspeaking students. *Augmentative and Alternative Communication, 4* (1), 23–34.

Pino, O. (2000). The effect of context on mother's interaction style with Down's syndrome and typically developing children. *Research in Developmental Disabilities, 21,* 329–346.

Poulson, C. L. (1988). Operant conditioning of vocalization rate of infants with Down syndrome. *American Journal on Mental Retardation, 93,* 57–63.

Remington, B., & Clarke, S. (1993). Simultaneous communication and speech comprehension. Part 1: Comparison of two methods of teaching expressive signing and speech comprehension skills. *Augmentative and Alternative Communication, 9,* 36–48.

Remington, B., & Clarke, S. (1993). Simultaneous communication and speech comprehension. Part II: Comparison of two methods of overcoming selective attention during expressive sign training. *Augmentative and Alternative Communication, 9,* 49–60.

Rosales, R., & Rehfeldt, R. A. (2007). Contriving transitive conditioned establishing operations to establish derived manding skills in adults with severe developmental disabilities. *Journal of Applied Behavior Analysis, 40* (1), 105–121. doi: 10.1901/jaba.2007.117–05.

Salzberg, C. L., & Villani, T. V. (1983). Speech training by parents of Down syndrome toddlers: Generalization across settings and instructional contexts. *American Journal of Mental Deficiency, 87* (4), 403–413.

Sanz Aparicio, M. T., & Menéndez Balana, J. (2002). Early language stimulation of Down's syndrome babies: A study on the optimum age to begin. *Early Child Development and Care, 172,* 651–656. doi: 10.1080=0300443022000046886.

Sanz Aparicio, M. T., & Menéndez Balana, J. (2003). Social early stimulation of trisomy-21 babies. *Early Child Development and Care, 173* (5), 557–561. doi: 10.1080/0300443032000088221.

Schlosser, R. W., Belfiore, P. J., Nigam, R., Blischak, D., & Hetzroni, O. (1995). The effects of speech output technology in the learning of graphic symbols. *Journal of Applied Behavior Analysis, 28* (4), 537–549.

Schwartz, I. S., Garfinkle, A. N., & Bauer, J. (1998). The Picture Exchange Communication System: Communicative outcomes for young children with disabilities. *Topics in Early Childhood Special Education, 18* (3), 144–159.

Sigafoos, J., Doss, S., & Reichle, J. (1989). Developing mand and tact repertoires in persons with severe developmental disabilities using graphic symbols. *Research in Developmental Disabilities, 10,* 183–200.

Sigafoos, J., Green, V. A., Payne, D., Son, S., O'Reilly, M., & Lancioni, G. E. (2009). A comparison of picture exchange and speech-generating devices: Acquisition, preference, and effects on social interaction. *Augmentative and Alternative Communication, 25* (2), 99–109. doi: 10.1080/07434610902739959.

Taubman, M., Brierley, S., Wishner, J., Baker, D., McEachin, J., & Leaf, R. B. (2001). The effectiveness of a group discrete trial instructional approach for preschoolers with developmental disabilities. *Research in Developmental Disabilities, 22,* 205–219.

Tekin-Iftar, E. (2003). Effectiveness of peer delivered simultaneous prompting on teaching community signs to students with developmental disabilities. *Education and Training in Developmental Disabilities, 38* (1), 77–94.

Thompson, R. H., Cotnor-Bichelman, N. M., McKerchar, P. M., Tate, T. L., & Dancho, K. A. (2007). Enhancing early communication through infant sign training. *Journal of Applied Behavior Analysis, 40* (1), 15–23.

Tirapelle, L., & Cipani, E. (1991). Developing functional requesting: Acquisition, durability, and generalization of effects. *Exceptional Child, 58* (3), 260–269.

Valentino, A. L., Shillingsburg, M. A., & Call, N. A. (2012). Comparing the effects of echoic prompts and echoic prompts plus modeled prompts on intraverbal behavior. *Journal of Applied Behavior Analysis, 45* (2), 431–435. doi:10.1901/jaba.2012.45–431.

Warren, S. F. (1992). Facilitating basic vocabulary acquisition with milieu teaching procedures. *Journal of Early Intervention, 16,* 235–251.

Warren, S. F., Yoder, P. J., Gazdag, G. E., Kim, K., & Jones, H. A. (1993). Facilitating prelinguistic communication skills in young children with developmental delay. *Journal of Speech and Hearing Research, 36,* 83–97.

Welch, S. J., & Pear, J. J. (1980). Generalization of naming responses to objects in the natural environment as a function of training stimulus modality with retarded children. *Journal of Applied Behavior Analysis, 13* (4), 629–643.

Wilkinson, K. M., & Albert, A. (2001). Adaptation of fast mapping for vocabulary intervention with augmented language users. *Augmentative and Alternative Communication, 17,* 120–132.

Wright, J., & Cashdan, A. (1989). Teaching expressive language to a non-speaking child with Down's syndrome: Classroom applications. *Child Language Teaching and Therapy, 5,* 33–48.

Wright, C. A., Kaiser, A. P., Reikowsky, D. I., & Roberts, M. Y. (2013). Effects of a naturalistic sign intervention on expressive language of toddlers with Down syndrome. *Journal of Speech, Language, and Hearing Research, 56* (3), 994–1008. doi:10.1044/1092–4388(2012/12–0060)994.

Yoder, P. J., & Warren, S. F. (2002). Effects of prelinguistic milieu teaching and parent responsivity education on dyads involving children with intellectual disabilities. *Journal of Speech, Language, and Hearing Research, 45* (6), 1158–1174.

Yoder, P., Woynaroski, T., Fey, M., & Warren, S. (2014). Effects of dose frequency of early communication intervention in young children with and without Down syndrome. *American Journal on Intellectual and Developmental Disabilities, 119* (1), 17–32. doi:10.1352/1944-7558-119.1.17.

Cognitive Development

Dalton, A. J., Rubino, C. A., & Hislop, M. W. (1973). Some effects of token rewards on school achievement of children with Down's syndrome. *Journal of Applied Behavior Analysis, 6* (2), 251–259.

Estevez, A., Fuentes, L. J., Overmier, J. B., & Gonzalez, C. (2003). Differential outcomes effect in children and adults with Down Syndrome. *American Journal on Mental Retardation, 108* (2), 108–116.

Farb, J., & Throne, J. M. (1978). Improving the generalized mnemonic performance of a Down's syndrome child. *Journal of Applied Behavior Analysis, 11* (3), 413–419.

Kennedy, E. J., & Flynn, M. C. (2003). Training phonological awareness skills in children with Down syndrome. *Research in Developmental Disabilities, 24,* 44–57.

McBride, B. J., & Schwartz, I. S. (2003). Effects of teaching early interventionists to use discrete trials during ongoing classroom activities. *Topics in Early Childhood Special Education, 23* (1), 5–17.

Pasnak, R., Whitten, J. C., Perry, P., Waiss, S., Madden, S. E., & Watson-White, S. A. (1995). Achievement gains after instruction on classification and seriation. *Education and Training in Mental Retardation and Developmental Disabilities, 30* (2), 109–117.

Pufpaff, L. A., Blischak, D. M., & Lloyd, L. L. (2000). Effects of modified orthography on the identification of printed words. *American Journal on Mental Retardation, 105* (1), 14–24.

Sloper, P., Glenn, S. M., & Cunningham, C. C. (1986). The effect of intensity of training on sensori-motor development in infants with Down's syndrome. *Journal of Mental Deficiency Research, 30*, 149–162.

Stith, L. E, & Fishbein, H. D. (1996). Basic money-counting skills of children with mental retardation. *Research in Developmental Disabilities, 17* (3), 185–201.

Throne, J. M., & Farb, J. (1978). Can mental retardation be reversed? *The British Journal of Mental Subnormality, 2* (47), 67–73.

Wilkinson, K. M., & Albert, A. (2001). Adaptation of fast mapping for vocabulary intervention with augmented language users. *Augmentative and Alternative Communication, 17*, 120–132.

Self-Care Skills

Averink, M., Melein, L., & Duker, P. C. (2005). Establishing diurnal bladder control with the response restriction method: Extended study on its effectiveness. *Research in Developmental Disabilities, 26*, 143–151. doi:10.1016/j.ridd.2004.02.001.

Biederman, G. B., Fairhall, J. L., Raven, K. A., & Davey, V. A. (1998). Verbal prompting, hand-over-hand instruction, and passive observation in teaching children with developmental disabilities. *Exceptional Children, 64* (4), 503–511.

Bonser, S. M., & Belfiore, P. J. (2001). Strategies and considerations for teaching an adolescent with Down syndrome and type 1 diabetes to self-administer insulin. *Education and Training in Mental Retardation and Developmental Disabilities, 36* (1), 94–102.

DeLeon, I. G., Hagopian, L. P., Rodriquez-Catter, V., Bowman, L. G, Long, E. S., & Boelter, E. W. (2008). Increasing wearing of prescription glasses in individuals with mental retardation. *Journal of Applied Behavior Analysis, 41* (1), 137–142. doi: 10.1901/jaba.2008.41-137.

Gibbons, B. G., Williams, K. E., & Riegel, K. E. (2007). Reducing tube feeds and tongue thrust: Combining an oral-motor and behavioral approach to feeding. *The American Journal of Occupational Therapy, 61* (4), 384–391.

Griffen, A. K., Wolery, M., & Schuster, J. W. (1992). Triadic instruction of chained food preparation responses: Acquisition and observational learning. *Journal of Applied Behavior Analysis, 25* (1), 193–204.

Lancioni, G. E., Singh, N. N., O'Reilly, M. F., Sigafoos, J., Oliva, D., Smaldone, A., & Martire, M. L. (2009). Two persons with multiple disabilities use a mouth-drying response to reduce the effects of their drooling. *Research in Developmental Disabilities, 30*, 1229–1236. doi:10.1016/j.ridd.2009.04.007.

Mathews, J. R., Hodson, G. D., Crist, W. B., & LaRoche, G. R. (1992). Teaching young children to use contact lenses. *Journal of Applied Behavior Analysis, 25* (1), 229–235.

Mechling, L. C., & Gast, D. L. (1997). Combination audio/visual self-prompting system for teaching chained tasks to students with intellectual disabilities. *Education and Training in Mental Retardation and Developmental Disabilities, 32* (2), 138–153.

Sanz, M. T., & Menéndez, J. (2010). Parents' training: Effects of the self-help skills programme with Down's syndrome babies. *Early Child Development and Care, 180*, 735–742. doi: 10.1080/03004430802279918.

Shore, B. A., LeBlanc, D., & Simmons, J. (1999). Reduction of unsafe eating in a patient with esophageal stricture. *Journal of Applied Behavior Analysis, 32* (2), 225–228.

Behavior That Interferes with Learning

Anderson, C. M., & Long, E. S. (2002). Use of structured descriptive assessment methodology to identify variables affecting problem behavior. *Journal of Applied Behavior Analysis, 25* (2), 137–154.

Athens, E. S., Vollmer, T. R, Sloman, K. N., & St. Peter Pipkin, C. (2008). An analysis of vocal stereotypy and therapist fading. *Journal of Applied Behavior Analysis, 41* (2), 291–297. doi: 10.1901/jaba.2008.41-291.

Benoit, D. A., Edwards, R. P., Olmi, D. J., Wilczynski, S. M., & Mandal, R. L. (2001). Generalization of a positive treatment package for child noncompliance. *Child & Family Behavior Therapy, 23* (2), 19–32.

Borrero, J. C., Vollmer, T. R., Wright, C. S., Lerman, D. C., & Kelley, M. E. (2002). Further evaluation of the role of protective equipment in the functional analysis of self-injurious behavior. *Journal of Applied Behavior Analysis, 35* (1), 69–72.

Brooks, A., Todd, A. W., Tofflemoyer, S., & Horner, R. H. (2003). Use of functional assessment and a self-management system to increase academic engagement and work completion. *Journal of Positive Behavior Interventions, 5* (3), 144–152.

Camp, E. M., Iwata, B. A., Hammond, J. L., & Bloom, S. E. (2009). Antecedent versus consequent events as predictors of problem behavior. *Journal of Applied Behavior Analysis, 42* (2), 469–483. doi: 10.1901/jaba.2009.42-469

Cole, C. L., & Levinson, T. R. (2002). Effects of within-activity choices on the challenging behavior of children with severe developmental disabilities. *Journal of Positive Behavior Interventions, 4* (1), 29–37.

Derby, K. M., Wacker, D. P., Peck, S., Sasso, G., DeRaad, A., Berg, W., Asmus, J., & Ulrich, S. (1994). Functional analysis of separate topographies of aberrant behavior. *Journal of Applied Behavior Analysis, 27* (2), 267–278.

Doughty, S. S., Anderson, C. M., Doughty, A. H., Williams, D. C., & Saunders, K. J. (2007). Discriminative control of punished stereotyped behavior in humans. *Journal of the Experimental Analysis of Behavior, 87* (3), 325–336. doi: 10.1901/jeab.2007.39-05.

Duker, P. C., & Van den Munckhof, M. (2007). Heart rate and the role of the active receiver during contingent electric shock for severe self-injurious behavior. *Research in Developmental Disabilities, 28,* 43–49. doi:10.1016/j.ridd.2005.05.010.

Feeley, K. M., & Jones, E. A. (2006). Addressing challenging behaviour in children with Down syndrome: The use of applied behavior analysis for assessment and intervention. *Down Syndrome Research and Practice, 11* (2), 64–77.

Feeley, K. M., & Jones, E. A. (2008). Preventing challenging behaviours in children with Down syndrome: Attention to early developing repertoires. *Down Syndrome Research and Practice, 12,* 11–14. doi:1 0.3104/reviews.2076.

Feeley, K. M., & Jones, E. A. (2008). Strategies to address challenging behaviour in young children with Down syndrome. *Down Syndrome Research and Practice, 12,* 153–163.

Feldman, M. A., & Werner, S. E. (2002). Collateral effects of behavioral parent training on families of children with developmental disabilities and behavior disorders. *Behavioral Interventions, 17,* 75–83. doi: 10.1002/bin.111.

Fisher, W. W., Piazza, C. C., Bowman, L. G., Hanley, G. P., & Adelinis, J. D. (1997). Direct and collateral effects of restraints and restraint fading. *Journal of Applied Behavior Analysis, 30* (1), 105–120.

Fisher, W. W., Bowman, L. G., Thompson, R.H., Contrucci, S. A., Burd, L., & Alon, G. (1998). Reductions in self-injury produced by transcutaneous electrical nerve stimulation. *Journal of Applied Behavior Analysis, 31* (93), 493–496.

Gardner, W. I., Cole, C. L., Berry, D. L., & Nowinski, J. M. (1983). Reduction of disruptive behaviors in mentally retarded adults: A self-management approach. *Behavior Modification, 7,* 76–96. doi: 10.1177/01454455830071006.

Green, V. A., O'Reilly, M. O., Itchon, J., & Sigafoos, J. (2005). Persistence of early emerging aberrant behavior in children with developmental disabilities. *Research in Developmental Disabilities, 26,* 47–55. doi:10.1016/j.ridd.2004.07.003.

Hagopian, L. P., Paclawskyj, T. R., & Contrucci Kuhn, S. (2005). The use of conditional probability analysis to identify a response chain leading to the occurrence of eye poking. *Research in Developmental Disabilities, 26,* 393–397. doi:10.1016/j.ridd.2003.09.002.

Hall, A. M., Neuharth-Pritchett, S., & Belfiore, P. J. (1997). Reduction of aggressive behaviors with changes in activity: Linking descriptive and experimental analyses. *Education and Training in Mental Retardation and Developmental Disabilities, 32* (4), 331–339.

Haring, T. G., & Kennedy, C. H. (1990). Contextual control of problem behavior in students with severe disabilities. *Journal of Applied Behavior Analysis, 23* (2), 235–243.

Hetzroni, O. E., & Roth, T. (2003). Effects of a positive support approach to enhance communicative behaviors of children with mental retardation who have challenging behaviors. *Education and Training in Developmental Disabilities, 38* (1), 95–105.

Iwata, B. A., Pace, G. M., Dorsey, M. F., Zarcone, J. R., Vollmer, T. R., Smith, R. G., Rodgers, T. A., Lerman, D. C., Shore, B. A., Mazaleski, J. L., Goh, H., Edwards Cowdery, G., Kalsher, M. J., McCosh, K. C., & Willis, K. D. (1994). The functions of self-injurious behavior: An experimental-epidemiological analysis. *Journal of Applied Behavior Analysis, 27* (2), 215–240.

Iwata, B. A., Dorsey, M. F., Slifer, K. J., Bauman, K. E., & Richman, G. S. (1994). Toward a functional analysis of self-injury. *Journal of Applied Behavior Analysis, 27* (2), 197–209.

Lalli, J. S., Browder, D. M., Mace, F. C., & Brown, D. K. (1993). Teacher use of descriptive analysis data to implement interventions to decrease students' problem behaviors. *Journal of Applied Behavior Analysis, 26* (2), 227–238.

Mace, F. C., Hock, M. L., Lalli, J. S., West, B. J., Belfiore, P., Pinter, E., & Kirby Brown, D. (1988). Behavioral momentum in the treatment of noncompliance. *Journal of Applied Behavior Analysis, 21* (2), 123–141.

Magee, S. K., & Ellis, J. (2001). The detrimental effects of physical restraint as a consequence for inappropriate classroom behavior. *Journal of Applied Behavior Analysis, 34* (4), 501–504.

Marcus, B. A., & Vollmer, T. R. (1996). Combining noncontingent reinforcement and differential reinforcement schedules as treatment for aberrant behavior. *Journal of Applied Behavior Analysis, 29* (1), 43–51.

Marcus, B. A., & Vollmer, T. R. (1995). Effects of differential negative reinforcement on disruption and compliance. *Journal of Applied Behavior Analysis, 28* (2), 229–230.

Marcus, B. A., Vollmer, T. R., Swanson, V., Roane, H. R., & Ringdahl, J. E. (2001). An experimental analysis of aggression. *Behavior Modification, 25,* 189–213. doi: 10.1177/0145445501252002.

Matson, J. L., & Dempsey, T. (2009). The nature and treatment of compulsions, obsessions, and rituals in people with developmental disabilities. *Research in Developmental Disabilities, 20,* 603–611. doi:10.1016/j.ridd.2008.10.001.

Mazaleski, J. L, Iwata, B. A., Vollmer, T. R., Zarcone, J. R., & Smith, R. G. (1993). Analysis of the reinforcement and extinction components in DRO contingencies with self-injury. *Journal of Applied Behavior Analysis, 26* (2), 143–156.

McAdam, D. B., Sherman, J. A., Sheldon, J. B., & Napolitano, D. A. (2004). Behavioral interventions to reduce the pica of persons with developmental disabilities. *Behavior Modification, 28,* 45–72. doi: 10.1177/0145445503259219.

McComas, J. J., Thompson, A., & Johnson, L. (2003). The effects of presession attention on problem behavior maintained by different reinforcers. *Journal of Applied Behavior Analysis, 36* (3), 297–307.

McDonald, M. R., & Budd, K. S. (1983). "Booster shots" following didactic parent training: Effects of follow-up using graphic feedback and instructions. *Behavior Modification, 7,* 211–223.

Millichap, D., Oliver, C., McQuillan, S., Kalsy, S., Lloyd, V., & Hall, S. (2003). Descriptive functional analysis of behavioral excesses shown by adults with Down syndrome and dementia. *International Journal of Geriatric Psychiatry, 18,* 844–854.

Neil, N. N., & Jones, E. A. (2016). Repetitive behavior in children with Down syndrome: Functional analysis and intervention. *Journal of Developmental and Physical Disabilities, 28* (2), 267–288. doi: 10.1007/s10882-015-9465-x.

O'Reilly, M. F., Murray, N., Lancioni, G. E., Sigafoos, J., & Lacey, C. (2003). Functional analysis and intervention to reduce self-injurious and agitated behavior when removing protective equipment for brief time periods. *Behavior Modification, 27,* 538–559. doi: 10.1177/0145445503255573.

Oliver, C., Hall, S., & Nixon, J. (1999). A molecular to molar analysis of communicative and problem behaviors. *Research in Developmental Disabilities, 20* (3), 197–213.

Plant, K. M., & Sanders, M. R. (2007). Reducing problem behavior during care-giving in families of preschool-aged children with developmental disabilities. *Research in Developmental Disabilities, 28,* 362–385. doi:10.1016/j.ridd.2006.02.009.

Rapp, J. T., Vollmer, T. R., St. Peter Pipkin, C., Dozier, C. L., & Cotnoir, N. M. (2004). Analysis of response allocation in individuals with multiple forms of stereotyped behavior. *Journal of Applied Behavior Analysis, 37* (4), 481–501.

Repp, A. C., & Karsh, K. G. (1994). Hypothesis-based interventions for tantrum behaviors of persons with developmental disabilities in school settings. *Journal of Applied Behavior Analysis, 27* (1), 21–31.

Ringdahl, J. E., Call, N. A., Mews, J. B., Boelter, E. W., & Christensen, T. J. (2008). Assessment and treatment of aggressive behavior without a clear social function. *Research in Developmental Disabilities, 29*, 351–362. doi:10.1016/j.ridd.2007.06.003.

Romaniuk, C., Miltenberger, R., Conyers, C., Jenner, N., Jurgens, M., & Ringenberg, C. (2002). The influence of activity choice on problem behaviors maintained by escape versus attention. *Journal of Applied Behavior Analysis, 35* (4), 349–363.

Rosine, L. P. C., & Martin, G. L. (1983). Self-management training to decrease undesirable behavior of mentally handicapped adults. *Rehabilitation Psychology, 28* (4), 195–205.

Shaw, R., & Simms, T. (2009). Reducing attention-maintained behavior through the use of positive punishment, differential reinforcement of low rates, and response marking. *Behavioral Interventions, 24*, 249–263. doi: 10.1002/bin.287.

Smith, R. G., Iwata, B. A., Vollmer, T. R., & Zarcone, J. R. (1993). Experimental analysis and treatment of multiply controlled self-injury. *Journal of Applied Behavior Analysis, 26* (2), 183–196.

St. Peter Pipkin, C. C., Vollmer, T. R., Bourret, J. C., Borrero, C. S. W., Sloman, K. N., & Rapp, J. T. (2005). On the role of attention in naturally occurring matching relations. *Journal of Applied Behavior Analysis, 38* (4), 429–443. doi: 10.1901/jaba.2005.172-04.

Thompson, R. H., Iwata, B. A., Conners, J., & Roscoe, E. M. (1999). Effects of reinforcement for alternative behavior during punishment of self-injury. *Journal of Applied Behavior Analysis, 32* (3), 317–328.

Thompson, R. H., Iwata, B. A., Hanley, G. P., Dozier, C. L., & Samaha, A. L. (2003). The effects of extinction, noncontingent reinforcement, and differential reinforcement of other behavior as control procedures. *Journal of Applied Behavior Analysis, 36* (2), 221–238.

Vaughn, B. J., & Horner, R. H. (1997). Identifying instructional tasks that occasion problem behaviors and assessing the effects of student versus teacher choice among these tasks. *Journal of Applied Behavior Analysis, 30* (2), 299–312.

Vollmer, T. R., Marcus, B. A., Ringdahl, J. E., & Roane, H. S. (1995). Progressing from brief assessments to extended experimental analyses in the evaluation of aberrant behavior. *Journal of Applied Behavior Analysis, 28* (4), 561–576.

Zarcone, J. R., Iwata, B. A., Vollmer, T. R., Jagtiani, S., Smith, R. G., & Mazaleski, J. L. (1993). Extinction of self-injurious escape behavior with and without instructional fading. *Journal of Applied Behavior Analysis, 26* (3), 353–360.

Chapter 3

BEHAVIORALLY BASED INSTRUCTION

In this chapter, we help you become familiar with important terms and strategies that you will need as you implement this model of intervention. In Book 2 of this manual, we provide step-by-step procedures to teach skills and address behaviors that may interfere with learning. These procedures involve behavior analytic strategies that may be new to you. Thus, in addition to reading this chapter now, you will likely refer back to this chapter as you read Book 2 to refresh yourself on some of the terms and strategies. Are you ready to get started? We hope so!

Getting Started

To begin, we would like to introduce you to three young children with Down syndrome. They represent children with different needs and families who have different resources available to them as well as varying family goals. We will refer to these children and their programming at various ages in Books 1 and 2 of this manual.

Jeremy was a nine-month-old boy and his parents' only child. At the time, providing Jeremy with stimulation and encouraging him to explore his environment were very important to them. Jeremy watched toys that lit up and made sounds but rarely reached for them, and when he did, touched them for only a second or two. One of Jeremy's family's goals was for him to learn to reach and grasp toys and explore them.

Megan was three years old and the youngest of three children. She loved books and her dollhouse, listening to music, and interacting with adults. She attended a daycare three days each week at her father's place of work, and she spent the other days with her grandmother. Her parents and educational team created goals for Megan. One goal was expanding her understanding of things they were saying (referred to as receptive vocabulary).

Hannah was a four-year-old girl. She and her six-year-old brother lived with their mother. She enjoyed dancing, playing games on her iPad, and soccer. She attended her neighborhood preschool five half-days each week. One of her mother's goals was for Hannah to learn how to clean up after herself and help around the house—putting toys in the correct bins and shelves, her clothes in her dresser, and utensils in the correct slots in the drawer. These were all chores her mother had started teaching Hannah's older brother when he was four years old.

HOW TO TEACH NEW SKILLS

What Jeremy, Megan, and Hannah were learning are examples of *behaviors*. Because the children have not learned these behaviors yet, they are being targeted for change and are referred to as **target behaviors**. Based on their parents' goals, here is how we would express the target behaviors:

JEREMY ~ Target Behavior. Reach and grasp a toy using his whole hand (called a *palmar grasp*).

MEGAN ~ Target Behavior. Identify things in her environment about which her family and teacher are talking.

HANNAH ~ Target Behavior. Clean up, such as by putting her cars in a basket or her socks in a drawer when asked to do so.

A Learning Opportunity: The Three-Term Contingency

Each time a child has an opportunity to engage in a target behavior, it is considered a **learning opportunity**. Here are the learning opportunities identified for Jeremy, Megan, and Hannah:

JEREMY ~ Learning Opportunity. When there was a toy within reach and Jeremy reached for and grasped it, he could feel the soft fabric and shake the toy to hear the sounds it made.

MEGAN ~ Learning Opportunity. When her teacher named things in her environment and Megan pointed to, touched them, or picked them up, her teacher said, "Great job," and often gave her a favorite toy.

HANNAH ~ Learning Opportunity. When Hannah's mother asked her to clean up, Hannah cleaned up, and her mother thanked her and gave her a big hug.

You might not have thought of these scenarios as learning opportunities, but they are, and parents and other caregivers present learning opportunities throughout daily interactions with their children. Learning occurs when three things are in place, referred to as the *three-term contingency*. The components of the three-term contingency are:

- **Antecedent**—a *stimulus* (an item, event, or some change in the environment) that occurs immediately *before* a behavior occurs. Antecedents may include spoken words (e.g., someone saying, "Hello" or "Come here," or asking a question), written words (e.g., a list of chores or a sign for the boys' or girls' restroom), or even something as subtle as an untied shoe or a box of favorite cookies.
- **Behavior**—what the child does (i.e., the action or skill performed by the child) in the presence of the antecedent. A *response* is one instance of a behavior. Behavior is always observable, which means we can see and/or hear it.
- **Consequence**—another stimulus (an item, event, or some change in the environment), but this one occurs *after* the child's behavior.

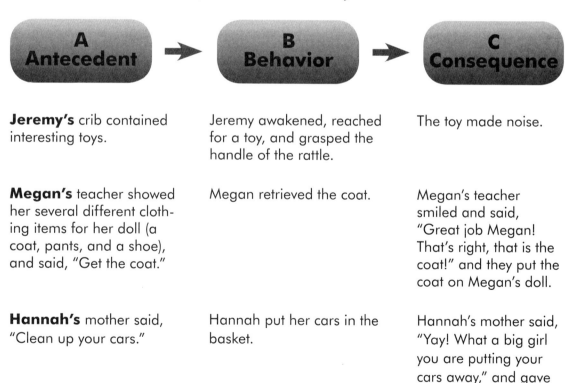

A Antecedent	B Behavior	C Consequence
Jeremy's crib contained interesting toys.	Jeremy awakened, reached for a toy, and grasped the handle of the rattle.	The toy made noise.
Megan's teacher showed her several different clothing items for her doll (a coat, pants, and a shoe), and said, "Get the coat."	Megan retrieved the coat.	Megan's teacher smiled and said, "Great job Megan! That's right, that is the coat!" and they put the coat on Megan's doll.
Hannah's mother said, "Clean up your cars."	Hannah put her cars in the basket.	Hannah's mother said, "Yay! What a big girl you are putting your cars away," and gave her a hug and kiss.

In each of the examples, notice how the antecedent occurred first, followed by the behavior. Also, notice that what is described as the consequences would be considered pleasurable events from the children's perspectives. When a child experiences a pleasurable event after a behavior, it is likely that he will continue to engage in that behavior. This is how children learn.

Advanced Information ➔ More about Applied Behavior Analysis

We have not included a comprehensive and complete description of every term and strategy in applied behavior analysis in this chapter. Rather, we selected the terms and strategies that you will be using most often. There are several ways that you can learn about additional strategies: through textbooks on applied behavior analysis and professional journals that publish research reports about the use of behavior analytic interventions (see the previous chapter for additional information about journals), as well as online and in-person training opportunities. You can find information about these types of resources in Appendix B of this book.

What Is the Antecedent in Each Learning Opportunity?

An antecedent is any event that comes before a behavior. It can be visual (e.g., seeing toys on the floor), auditory (e.g., hearing directions given by the teacher), olfactory (e.g., smelling cookies), and even tactile (e.g., a tap on the arm). Children experience many antecedent stimuli throughout the day, but certainly do not react to all of those stimuli. In general, we react to the stimuli that are associated with pleasurable events.

JEREMY ~ Antecedent in Each Learning Opportunity. Upon seeing a favorite toy in his crib, Jeremy reached for and grasped it. He did so because, on previous occasions when he reached and grasped, he got to hear the funny noise the toy made.

MEGAN ~ Antecedent in Each Learning Opportunity. Megan's teacher said, "Get the coat," and Megan responded by picking up the coat. She did so because, before, when she picked that clothing item in response to her teacher's instruction, it resulted in her teacher smiling and saying nice things and putting the coat on her doll to continue playing.

Notice that in each of these examples something pleasurable happened after the child engaged in the response. There was a funny noise when Jeremy reached and grasped the toy, and Megan's teacher gave her a big smile and said nice things after she picked up the coat. When the consequence that occurs after the behavior *increases* the likelihood that behavior will occur again, it is referred to as **reinforcement**. Remember, we introduced the term briefly in Chapter 2. Reinforcement occurs when a specific event or object follows a response and increases the likelihood of that behavior occurring again.

Now, when a behavior occurs and reinforcement follows, the particular stimulus that was present before the behavior is a **discriminative stimulus** (abbreviated as S^D). This means that, in the presence of that antecedent, the behavior is likely to occur because the child has learned that good things will follow. So, for Jeremy, the toy becomes the S^D for reaching and grabbing because in the past doing so resulted in the toy making noise. And the teacher's direction to "Get the coat" is the S^D for Megan to select the coat because in the past she received smiles and praise from her teacher after she got the coat.

This is how all three components of a learning opportunity work together: an S^D results in behavior that in turn results in reinforcement.

Remember, learning will occur when we have three things:
1. antecedent (S^D),
2. person's behavior, and
3. consequence that reinforces the person's behavior.

A learning opportunity involves each of the components of the three-term contingency. When opportunities are presented several times within a specific time frame, together they are referred to as a **teaching session**. A child is likely to acquire a skill when there are repeated opportunities presented within a session and when sessions are repeated several times throughout a day or a week.

Teaching Skills to Be Used in Different Situations: Generalization

When identifying learning opportunities, it is important to remember that you want your child to be able to use the behavior (or skill) in many different situations. When a child performs a skill in different situations, it is referred to as **generalization.**

JEREMY ~ Generalization. Jeremy's caregivers included his parents and grandparents, who taught him to reach for different types of toys in his crib (a plush toy, small musical toy, etc.). He reached for things in many different places in the house (while on the blanket in the living room, sitting in his car seat, and in his stroller) and even at his grandparents' house.

MEGAN ~ Generalization. Megan's parents and teacher taught Megan to understand when they said "Coat" while playing with her dolls but also practiced with pictures of clothing items and even Megan's own clothes to make sure Megan correctly identified a variety of coats in different forms (e.g., pictures, real coats, small- and large-size coats, etc.).

HANNAH ~ Generalization. Hannah's mother said, "Clean up your cars" and sometimes changed the instruction, for example, saying, "Tidy up the cars" and "Put your cars away," and Hannah responded in the same way (i.e., she put her cars in the correct basket). Hannah even cleaned up when her teacher asked her to put away her toys at school.

Jeremy, Megan, and Hannah showed a type of generalization called *stimulus generalization.* Stimulus generalization occurs when a child performs a given skill in the presence of different stimuli (different items, events, people, or environments) than those that were used when he learned the skill. We constantly use skills we have learned in new situations, such as when we apply our math skills to figure out a store discount or when we drive a new car. As you think about teaching a specific skill, be sure to think about all the people with whom your child needs to be able to use the skill, the materials he must be able to use, and the places where he needs to be able to do the skill. Consider having all your child's caregivers present opportunities, in different places, and with different materials.

Teaching Your Child When It Is Appropriate to Perform the Behavior

The previous examples of generalization were all situations in which the target behaviors were appropriate and should occur. But there are also situations in which children should *not* engage in particular behaviors. For example, when Megan was first learning to identify a coat, she picked any article of clothing as a "coat." Thus, when her teacher said, "Get the hat," Megan would get the coat. This is an example of *overgeneralization*, which means a child performs a behavior in situations in which he should not. Now, you have learned that a stimulus that should lead to engaging in a certain response is referred to as discriminative stimulus (S^D). A stimulus that should *not* result in a certain response is referred to as *stimulus delta* (S-Delta; $S^\triangle$). Here is an example. The S^D for answering the phone is the phone ringing; the $S^\triangle$ is a silent phone.

For some children, teaching when they should *not* engage in a response is as important as teaching when they should. These are sometimes referred to as "do it" and "don't do it" opportunities for behavior. For example, children learn they can talk loudly outside on the playground but not in a movie theater or at the dinner table. They also learn that we answer the phone when it rings but not when it is not ringing. When your child engages in a response in the presence of some stimuli and not others, he is discriminating between the stimuli, which is referred to as *stimulus discrimination*.

MEGAN ~ Stimulus Discrimination. Megan's teacher showed Megan several different clothing items, each of which functioned as a stimulus. When Megan's teacher said, "Get the coat," that direction *and* the coat itself should function as the S^D for selecting the coat. Each of the other stimuli (the hat, pants, shoes, and shirt) were $S^\triangle$s, because those items should not be associated with the delivery of reinforcement when her teacher said, "Get the coat." Early on, Megan was also picking the coat when her teacher asked her to get the other items. She was experiencing a problem with *stimulus control.* That is, the important antecedent stimuli were not *controlling* her responses (i.e., the S^D "Get the hat" was not accurately controlling her response). To address this, Megan's teacher presented some learning opportunities for her to get a coat along with some learning opportunities to get other items in her environment (i.e., opportunities when she should *not* choose the coat and instead get another item). When Megan learned to get other items (not the coat) when asked, her behavior was under stimulus control.

JEREMY ~ Stimulus Discrimination. Jeremy learned to reach and touch many different toys in his crib, the living room, and his grandparents' house. But, he also started reaching and touching the cat food bowls. This was a "don't do it" opportunity. Jeremy's parents and grandparents made sure to interrupt any attempts Jeremy made to reach and touch the cat bowls.

When you teach your child, you will present both types of opportunities—those that should result in the child engaging in a target response and those that should not. This will help prevent overgeneralization and teach your child to discriminate between those situations.

Here are examples of "do it" and "don't do it" learning opportunities to consider when teaching a child to greet people by saying hi. "Do it" opportunities include:

- greeting peers as they enter the classroom in the morning
- greeting familiar teachers/therapists (e.g., speech therapist, occupational therapist, etc.)
- greeting familiar individuals on his street, at the library, or in the grocery store

"Don't do it" opportunities include:

- seeing a classmate again only five minutes after having already greeted him or her
- leaving a session with one of the therapists
- encountering people on the street, in the library, or grocery store who the child does not know

Advanced Information ➞ Another Type of Generalization

Another type of generalization is called **response generalization.** Response generalization occurs when the child engages in different behaviors in response to the same stimulus and all those behaviors work the same way or serve the same purpose. In an everyday example, in response to a server's question, "May I take your order?" we could respond very differently (but get the same result) by saying, "Burger and fries" or, "I would like a burger and small fries, please."

Jeremy ~ Response Generalization. After Jeremy learned to reach and grasp, his family taught him to manipulate and explore objects by pressing buttons and shaking them. Once he learned to press buttons and shake toys, he also explored objects in other ways by banging, dropping, and pushing. All these different ways of exploring objects resulted in interesting sights and sounds.

Megan ~ Response Generalization. Megan identified coats by touching the coat, handing the coat to her teacher, or pointing at the coat. No matter which way Megan identified the coat, her teacher responded with praise, saying, "Great job! That's the coat."

Hannah ~ Response Generalization. Hannah's mother taught her to clean up by putting her cars in a basket. Hannah also cleaned up by putting books on the shelf and blocks in the toy box. These different responses all resulted in Hannah's play things being put away and her mother's attention and praise for cleaning up.

Now you have learned about both types of generalization: stimulus generalization and response generalization. Both types of generalization are goals when teaching children skills.

How to Ensure Your Child Responds Correctly

If your child responds correctly to an antecedent (S^D) in an instructional setting, pleasurable events will follow. But, how do you ensure that your child responds correctly during the learning opportunity (and then receives reinforcement for doing so)? This is where **prompting strategies** come in. We provide prompts at the beginning of instruction to help children engage in a correct response. Prompting is used to increase the likelihood that your child engages in the target behavior. Once your child engages in the behavior, reinforcement can occur, which results in an increase in the behavior—that is learning!

Over time, we fade prompts (gradually stop using them), because our ultimate goal is for your child to perform the behavior on his own, without any assistance (i.e., without any prompts). This is independent performance—which is our goal!

Types of Prompts

There are two broad types of prompts that we use during intervention: response prompts and stimulus prompts.

Response Prompts

When prompts are directed at your child and guide him to produce a correct response, they are referred to as **response prompts**. When you physically help your child, or show him what to do, you are using response prompts, because what you are doing is directed at your child. There are three types of response prompts: verbal, physical, and modeling prompts.

Verbal prompts are spoken instructions, directions, or hints to help your child engage in the correct response. Adults often use verbal prompts to help children learn (e.g., saying, "Put the toothpaste on," then, "Brush," then, "Rinse," etc., to help a child brush his teeth or, "Where do you think that goes?" as a hint to put the toothbrush away).

HANNAH ~ Verbal Prompt. After she said, "Clean up your cars," Hannah's mother gave Hannah more specific instructions such as, "Pick up the car and put it in the basket," and then, "Now, pick up another car and put it in the basket." Each of these specific instructions served as a prompt for Hannah to clean up her cars.

Physical prompts consist of physical contact to guide your child to perform the correct response. We often provide assistance to our children to engage in a behavior (e.g., helping them put on their coats, shoes, and mittens on a winter day). This type of assistance is called a physical prompt because the adult places his or her hands over the child's hands while providing a great deal of assistance to complete the task. This is referred to as *hand-over-hand prompting,* one type of physical prompt.

JEREMY ~ Physical Prompt. To help Jeremy reach and grasp, his parents and grandparents picked up Jeremy's hand, brought it out toward the toy, and wrapped his hand around the toy to grasp it.

Modeling prompts involve showing your child exactly what you want him to do. For example, if you want him to bang a toy drum, you demonstrate it by banging the drum yourself. You might even say something such as, "Do it this way" while performing the model (this pairs a model prompt with a verbal prompt). If your child responds by imitating you (i.e., banging the drum), the model functions as a prompt for your child to respond correctly.

Models can be actions or words. If you want your child to perform an action, the model will be an action. For example, when a teacher tells the class, "Everyone, clap your hands," a student observes his peer put her hands together and clap (the model of the action). The student may then begin to clap too. If you want your child to say something, you can provide a *verbal model prompt.* For example, if you are teaching your child to say, "Good morning," each time a family member gets up in the morning, you provide a model for your child by saying, "Good morning." Model prompts may be provided by caregivers or peers (e.g., friends, family members, classmates).

Model prompts can be live or on video. Video modeling involves showing your child a video that demonstrates what he is supposed to do. You may have experience using video models if you have ever viewed a video on the Internet to make a new recipe or fix a household appliance. There are many online resources that have prerecorded video segments that can be used as models. For example, *Watch Me Learn* uses video-modeling techniques to help children learn appropriate social, language, and functional skills (http://www.watchmelearn.com/) and has its own YouTube channel (https://www.youtube.com/c/watchmelearn/videos).

Smartphones and tablets make it quite easy to create and show your own videos. This allows you to specifically tailor the video model to the target behavior and your child with either your child himself or another person (preferably a same-age peer) performing the desired behavior. Once you have created the video model, show your child the video just before (or sometimes just after) you present the S^D to prompt him to respond.

> **HELPFUL HINT**   **Will Your Child Respond to a Model Prompt?**
> A model prompt will only be effective if your child imitates what you do. Does your child imitate? If not, be sure to refer to the sections of Book 2, Chapters 2 through 5, that contain procedures for teaching imitation skills. If you are not sure if your child imitates, just model a few behaviors while saying, "Do this," to see if he will imitate you. For example, say, "Do this," while you clap your hands. Then do the same while tapping your leg or putting your arms up. Be sure not to say, "Clap your hands" or "Tap your leg," as then it will be hard to determine if your child is imitating your action or following your verbal direction. For verbal responses, say, "Say [sound, word, phrase]" to see if your child will imitate what you say.

Stimulus Prompts

When prompts are directed at antecedent stimuli (stimuli that occur before the response), they are referred to as *stimulus prompts*. Stimulus prompts help direct the child's attention to a particular aspect of the stimulus. This increases the likelihood that the child will produce a correct response. There are several types of stimulus prompts: movement, position, and picture/textual prompts.

Movement prompts are gestures such as pointing, leaning toward something, or tilting your chin toward something to help your child respond correctly to your instructions. While we may not give it much thought, we frequently point at things to help others understand what we want them to do. For example, while dining out, you might say, "Pass the salt" while pointing to the saltshaker across the table; this is a movement prompt.

MEGAN ~ Movement prompt. Megan's teacher and parents pointed to the coat to prompt Megan to choose the coat from a variety of other items when asked. In this case the movement prompt was a gesture, sometimes also referred to as a *gestural prompt*.

Position prompts just mean that you place the correct choice closer to the child so he will make the right response. This works because children are inclined to select the item closest to them. For example, if you are teaching a child to identify a square, you might position the square closer to him than the triangle and then ask, "Which one is the square?" (See photos at top of next page.)

Example of child responding correctly with (left) and without (right) a position prompt.

Visual prompts include pictures (graphics, drawings, photos, etc.) or text (words your child is able to read, referred to as **textual prompts**) added to the environment to help the child perform a specific behavior. Examples of visual prompts you might use include placing a sticky note on the refrigerator to remind you to get something from the grocery store or leaving out the empty box of garbage bags to remind you to get more from the basement. In school a photo of a trash can was used to prompt a child to clean up after snack. Seeing the photo of the trash can as he finished eating functioned as a prompt for him to place the napkin and paper cup in the trash can.

Written words can be paired with pictures or used alone to prompt a child to complete tasks. (See photo of chore list.) Written words can also be used to prompt your child to say something. When used this way, such prompts are referred to as **scripts.** For example, one mother wanted to teach her child to answer in a full sentence when asked, "What snack do you want?" She showed him an index card that said, "I want chips, please" (see photo).

HELPFUL HINT **What Can Be Used as a Visual Prompt?**

A simple search for "images of [what you are looking for]" in your browser will usually turn up a number of pictures you might use. Visual prompts can even be parts of the item to which they refer. For example, during snack time, a teacher wanted a child to say, "Juice." She used the label from the juice box as a prompt. When asked, "What do you want for snack today?" she showed the child the label from the juice box.

Considerations When Choosing a Type of Prompt

Once you know a particular prompt is effective, stick with it. If your child is resistant to a specific type of prompt (e.g., physical prompts), try a different one. You will make more progress if your prompting strategy does not cause any additional problems.

The type of skill you are teaching is an important factor to consider in deciding what type of prompt to use:

- When teaching a motor skill, a model prompt can be effective (if your child imitates). If the motor movements are not in your child's repertoire or your child does not imitate, use a physical prompt to guide him.
- When teaching a verbal skill, a picture or textual prompt (printed word) can help your child with exactly what he should say.
- When teaching your child to imitate, provide the model and then use a physical prompt to make sure he imitates your exact model. When teaching verbal imitation, pair a gesture or visual with a verbal model.
- When teaching a skill with many steps such as brushing teeth, visual cues can be used to remind your child to perform every step of the skill (e.g., a little booklet or a strip with photos indicating the steps).
- When teaching a skill that involves demonstrating an understanding of a concept or specific word (a receptive language skill), stimulus prompts such as positional or movement prompts may be effective. For example, if you want your child to show, point, or touch a specific color, shape, or word, you can move the correct response closer to your child or gesture toward the item.

Although verbal prompts can help your child respond correctly in many situations, in general we suggest you *not* use verbal prompts. Most children can learn efficiently without verbal prompting. Here are some reasons to avoid using verbal prompts:

- Verbal prompts can be difficult to fade.

  - ➤ Young children may enjoy the interaction and attention inherent in verbal prompts. From the child's perspective, why perform the task independently if a favorite person will "talk" him through it? Remember, we want to save pleasurable experiences for *after* the child performs the skill.

  - ➤ The child never has an opportunity to respond to the naturally occurring S^D without the prompt. We often see this in classroom settings where there are several support personnel (classroom aides or teaching assistants). After the classroom teacher gives directions, support staff often repeat the directions and then provide reinforcement when the child responds. Thus, the child begins to wait until the support person gives instructions rather than respond following the classroom teacher's directions (the naturally occurring S^D). The support person's instructions overshadow those of the teacher.

- Verbal prompts can be *very* intrusive. Imagine attending a workshop where someone provided verbal prompts through the whole presentation about how you should take notes. While the presenter spoke, the person prompted by saying, "Sit down, take out your paper, take out your pen, look at the screen, write that down, stop fidgeting, write that down too." This would be disruptive and probably annoying. Contrast this with a teacher who just subtly points or looks up to the screen when she wants to bring her student's attention to it. Students can rely on these types of subtle prompts, which often seem far more natural and less intrusive than verbal prompts.

- Consider what we know about strengths related to the Down syndrome behavioral phenotype. Strong visual processing means visual models may be very effective. Weaknesses in auditory short-term memory mean verbal prompts may actually not be very effective.

There are many ways you can help your child respond correctly. Once you have helped him respond with a prompt, you can work on having him do the behavior on his own, without your model, physical assistance, or visual prompt. This is referred to as **independent responding**, which occurs when we successfully fade prompts.

How to Fade Prompts to Ensure Your Child Responds Independently

Prompts are used to teach new skills and to promote the use of already learned skills, but it is important to fade prompts to enhance your child's independence. When you first start to teach a skill, it is the prompt that likely *controls* the behavior. That means the prompt has stimulus control over the behavior. But the goal is for the instruction or S^D to control the behavior. When we fade prompts, we are transferring stimulus control from the prompt to the S^D.

In an everyday example, think about what happens when you see a traffic light while driving. You stop when the light is red and go when the light is green. The red light has stimulus control over the behavior of putting your foot on the brake and stopping. Similarly, the green light has stimulus control over the behavior of putting your foot on the gas and speeding up. Now imagine a very nervous teenager whose very nervous father is teaching her to drive. As they approach a red light, the father says (i.e., delivers the verbal prompt), "Slow down—there is a red light ahead." The teenager then puts her foot on the brake. In this situation, what controls the teenager's behavior? If you answered the parent's verbal prompt, you would be correct. After lots of practice, the more confident teenager sees the red light and stops. In this situation, what controls the teenager's behavior? If you are thinking the red light, you are correct. In this situation, stimulus control has been transferred from the parent's prompt (saying, "Slow down—there is a red light ahead") to the naturally occurring stimulus (the red light), which enables the teenager to drive independently. This is exactly what you should be aiming for when teaching your child!

MEGAN ~ Responding Independently. Megan's teacher used a movement or gestural prompt (pointing to the correct item). Early on, it was not the teacher's words—"Get the coat"— that controlled the correct response (getting the coat), it was the teacher's point. When Megan began to respond to her teacher's instruction without the teacher having to point to the coat, she was responding independently to the S^D.

Most-to-Least Prompt Fading

When using prompts, we generally start by providing the most amount of assistance and then fade to the least amount of assistance. You may begin instruction by providing a prompt that involves the necessary assistance to reliably result in the child performing a specific behavior (referred to as the *most intrusive prompt*). This most intrusive prompt is individualized to your child, as it is the prompt that reliably helps your child engage in the correct response. When your child successfully responds when you provide the most intrusive prompt, begin to provide less and less intrusive prompts. A list of prompts from more intrusive to less intrusive is called a ***prompt hierarchy***. Moving from the most intrusive prompt to the least intrusive one is referred to as ***most-to-least prompt fading***.

Most-to-Least Prompt Fading of a Verbal Prompt.

Remember that the most intrusive prompt and the hierarchy will be individualized for your child. The most intrusive form of a verbal prompt might be to tell someone exactly what to do. Verbal prompts can be faded in length (e.g., using fewer words as part of the prompt) and volume (e.g., saying the words in a quieter voice).

HANNAH ~ Most-to-Least Prompt Fading of a Verbal Prompt. When she first taught Hannah to clean up, Hannah's mother used verbal prompts in the form of complete sentences (e.g., saying, "Pick up this car and put it in the basket"). This was the level of prompt that Hannah needed in order to perform the response (cleaning up her toys). Her mom faded these prompts (from the most intrusive verbal prompt to the least intrusive) by decreasing the length of the utterance (e.g. saying only part of the instruction such as, "Pick up this car and put…" and then just "Car").

Most-to-Least Prompt Fading of a Physical Prompt.

The most intrusive form of a physical prompt might be to hold the child's hand, arm, or other body part and physically guide him to make the desired response. Physical prompts become less intrusive as adults provide less physical assistance.

JEREMY ~ Most-to-Least Prompt Fading of Physical Prompts. When Jeremy's family taught him to reach for toys, they started with a full physical prompt (holding Jeremy's hand and arm, gently extending it, and wrapping his hand around the toy). As Jeremy successfully reached and grasped the toy, his family faded to a partial physical prompt in which they just touched Jeremy's elbow to guide him to reach and grasp the toy.

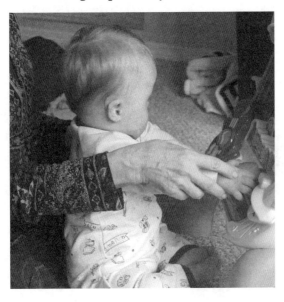 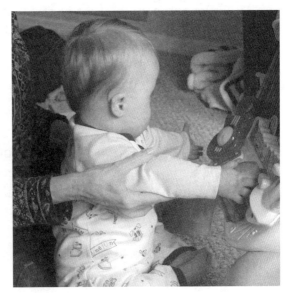

Jeremy's family implemented what is referred to as *graduated guidance.* The adults began with hand-over-hand guidance to help him complete a behavior and then moved the location of their hands to provide less guidance as he began to respond on his own. Note that Jeremy's family could have created a hierarchy with more steps to fade their physical prompt— for example, fading from a full physical to partial physical touching the child's wrist, then elbow, then shoulder. The hierarchy, including number of steps, will be individualized to the needs of your child.

Another type of fading is referred to as *shadowing*, which involves closely following the movements of the child, without making physical contact, moving your hands farther away to fade prompts.

Most-to-Least Prompt Fading of a Movement Prompt. The most intrusive form of a movement prompt might be to touch the object you want the child to choose and hold your finger on the object until the child makes a correct response. You could fade to less intrusive movement prompts by pointing at the object from an increasing distance or only quickly pointing to the object.

MEGAN ~ Most-to-Least Prompt Fading of a Movement Prompt. Megan's teacher used a movement prompt by pointing to the coat to prompt her to get the coat. When Megan successfully responded to this prompt, her teacher faded the movement prompt by placing her pointing finger farther away from the correct item (i.e., first three inches and then six inches away from the coat).

As the prompt was faded, Megan began to rely less on her teacher's pointing and began to attend to the actual coat and instruction to make the correct response. Eventually, the teacher did not point at all. She just said, "Get the coat," and Megan did so.

When Should You Fade a Prompt?

We keep saying you should fade your prompt when your child is "successful." But what does that mean? By success, we mean that your child is responding to the prompt with the correct behavior, not just one time, but several times. Remember, a learning opportunity consists of one S^D, a response (prompted or not), and a consequence. We often provide between five and ten opportunities (within a session) when teaching a specific skill. So criteria for success is often set at performing correctly on about 80 percent or more of the opportunities in a session across at least two consecutive sessions. Sometimes we also add across two days and two caregivers. The two sessions, days, and caregivers help ensure your child responds correctly at different times and with different people.

For some skills, it is important to set more stringent criteria. For example, safety skills such as crossing the street or not hugging strangers require 100 percent correct performance. There are also less vital skills such as saying hello to one's neighbors in passing that probably do not even need to be demonstrated 80 percent of the time.

Sometimes, fading a prompt results in the child engaging in an incorrect response. We discuss how to respond if your child makes an incorrect response or does not respond at all later in this chapter.

MEGAN ~ When to Fade a Prompt. Megan's mom presented several opportunities on Wednesday, and Megan performed correctly on more than 80 percent of them. The teacher then presented another session of multiple opportunities on Thursday, and again Megan performed correctly on more than 80 percent of them. That was more than 80 percent correct responding across two sessions, two days of instruction, and two caregivers. Now, on Friday, Megan's mom started to fade the prompt.

Another Way to Fade Prompts: Least-to-Most Prompt Fading

In almost all of the instructional programs in Book 2, we recommend using most-to-least prompt fading. However, there are other ways to fade prompts. *Least-to-most prompt fading* entails providing the least intrusive prompt first and, if the child does not respond or responds incorrectly, you give more assistance by providing a slightly more intrusive prompt. You continue to provide more assistance until the child performs the desired behavior, and then you provide reinforcement.

We do recommend using a least-to-most prompt fading strategy once your child has learned a skill but does not always do it correctly. In this case, you know your child has the skill in his repertoire because he has demonstrated success, but his performance is inconsistent. In this situation a less intrusive prompt may be just enough to get your child to respond correctly, and beginning with a more intrusive prompt is really unnecessary.

MEGAN ~ Least-to-Most Prompt Fading of a Movement Prompt. After teaching Megan to identify her coat when they said the word *coat*, her teacher and mother periodically checked whether Megan still identified her coat without a prompt. Now, they just said the word and waited. If Megan did not get her coat, then Megan's mother or teacher used a least-to-most prompting strategy: first pointing at the coat from six inches away, then three, and then touching it. So, they only used a more intrusive prompt when Megan made an error.

HELPFUL HINT **Choose Most-to-Least Prompt Fading When Teaching New Skills**

Prompt fading procedures are very important. When carefully chosen and implemented correctly, they lead to independent responding, and that is our goal. So, it is very important for you to understand how to choose between prompt fading strategies. Here is our favorite real-life example to illustrate the differences between most-to-least and least-to-most prompt fading strategies and why we begin with most-to-least prompt fading when teaching a new skill. When teaching a child to ride a bicycle, many parents start their children with training wheels, which we can consider the most intrusive prompt. Then, the training wheels come off, and typically an adult holds the handlebars and the back of the seat and runs alongside the child while he pedals. As the child gets better at riding, the adult pulls back the support, first letting go of the handlebars, then the seat, and then just running alongside the child. Of course, the adult begins by providing the most support; the child does not have the skill in his repertoire. If the adult started with the least intrusive prompt (running alongside the child), the child would likely fall off the bike. Thus, when a skill is *not* in the child's repertoire, it makes sense to start with a more intrusive prompt.

Deciding When to Use Most-to-Least or Least-to-Most Prompt Fading

Use most-to-least prompt fading:

✔ During the initial stages of teaching a new skill.

✔ When teaching a skill you think will be difficult for your child or for which your child has a history of difficulty.

Use least-to-most prompt fading:

✔ Once your child has the skill within his/her repertoire.

✔ If your child tends to be prompt dependent. For example, if your child has a tendency to wait for the prompt before responding, then, if you give a minimal prompt, he may respond.

Fading by Delaying the Delivery of the Prompt

Another very effective prompt fading strategy that we recommend throughout this manual is *time delay*. To implement a time delay procedure to fade prompts, you begin instruction by immediately prompting your child to make a correct response. This is referred to as a zero-second time delay, because you do not wait after the S^D—you deliver the prompt right away. Then, once the child is successful when prompted, introduce a pause or delay between the S^D and your prompt. This delay is initially only a few seconds long (two-second time delay, three-second time delay, etc.), but it gives the child a window of opportunity to make an independent response before you present the prompt. If your child responds within the time delay, then he has responded independently. If he does not respond within the time delay, prompt the correct response as soon as the time delay ends. This helps to ensure the child always responds correctly (and thus has the opportunity to practice the correct response on every opportunity).

A time delay can be used with both most-to-least and least-to-most prompt fading strategies.

- To use **most-to-least prompt fading with a time delay**, begin with a full prompt and fade to a partial prompt. Then, begin to implement the time delay procedure, introducing a partial prompt if your child does not respond by the end of the time delay interval.
- To use **least-to-most prompt fading with a time delay**, begin with a time delay and then use more intrusive prompts if your child does not respond at the end of the time delay.

JEREMY ~ Time Delay. Jeremy's family faded the physical prompt to reach for a toy to a light touch at Jeremy's elbow. They prompted him immediately following the S^D; that is, they used a zero-second time delay and Jeremy responded successfully. His parents and grandparents then introduced a five-second time delay. They presented a toy and waited five seconds. When Jeremy reached and grasped the toy within five seconds, his parent or grandparent paired praise with the consequences of reaching the toy and noted that Jeremy independently (that is, without a prompt) reached and grasped the toy. But, if after five seconds passed, Jeremy did not reach and grasp, his parent or grandparent touched his elbow (the last prompt that was used successfully to teach Jeremy to reach and grasp before they introduced the time delay). They made sure to note that Jeremy needed a prompt on those opportunities.

HELPFUL HINT **When Fading Prompts Remember...**
Remember, verbal prompts can be very intrusive and difficult to fade. Sometimes parents will fade from a physical prompt to a verbal prompt. We do not recommend this strategy and instead recommend fading *within* the type of prompt. For example, if you began by using a full physical prompt, fade to a partial physical, not a verbal prompt. If you began by using a

visual prompt, fade the prompt by making the picture smaller. If you find that the prompt you have chosen is not effective, take the time to carefully identify an effective prompt, develop a corresponding prompt hierarchy to fade within that type of prompt, and then systematically fade the prompt.

Delivering Consequences

Remember the three components of every learning opportunity: (1) an antecedent (S^D and prompt if necessary) to which (2) your child responds and then (3) a consequence. So, what should you do following your child's response? This will depend on how your child responds. Within instruction, there are three different ways your child can respond to the S^D (the antecedent):

- Your child can make a correct response (either independently or after a prompt).
- Your child can make an incorrect response (i.e., give or select the wrong answer). An incorrect response also includes situations in which your child engages in behavior that interferes with learning, as discussed at the end of this chapter and at more length throughout Book 2.
- Your child can not respond at all to the S^D.

During instruction, it is important for you to have a plan for how to respond in each of these three situations. This plan will be consistently implemented, just as your prompting procedures will be used consistently across learning opportunities.

What to Do When Your Child Responds Correctly

After your child responds correctly, you should provide a pleasurable consequence.

JEREMY ~ Consequence for a Correct Response. Jeremy reached and grasped a toy (correct response) and heard the funny noise it made (natural consequence). His parents and grandparents paired this with social attention. They praised him, saying, "What a big boy you are, Jeremy" and smiled brightly at him.

Carefully planning consequences will increase the likelihood your child will respond with the desired behavior again. Earlier, we introduced the term *reinforcement*, which is what happens when consequences increase the likelihood that a behavior will occur again in the future. Thus, the consequences that follow correct responses should function as reinforcers, because you want to see your child engage in those correct behaviors again. There are two different types of reinforcement—positive and negative—both of which increase the occurrence of behavior.

Positive Reinforcement

Positive reinforcement is the presentation of a consequence that increases the likelihood the behavior will occur in the future. The word *positive* (+) indicates that something is added to the environment. Objects (e.g., toys, food, or stickers) and activities (e.g., watching TV, swinging on a swing, or going for a walk) are examples of consequences that *may* function as positive reinforcers. *Social attention* is another example of positive reinforcement. This involves your interactions with your child in fun, loving ways—praise, hugs, kisses, smiles, and tickles are all examples of types of social attention that may be reinforcing to your child. Some activities involve social attention—finger plays, reading a book, or playing card games. Remember, for something to function as a reinforcer, it must result in an increase in the preceding behavior.

In the previous chapter, when we described the Down syndrome behavioral phenotype, we mentioned that social attention may be a particularly valuable reinforcer for your child with Down syndrome. Thus, it is highly likely that if you give your child social attention after he makes a desired response, he will make that response more often in the future.

MEGAN ~ Positive Reinforcement. When Megan identified a coat following the S^D "Get the coat," her teacher provided lots of social attention. She said, "Wow, you found the coat. It's such a pretty coat too." She then played with Megan, helping her put the coat on the doll. Since social attention and doll play were reinforcers for Megan, Megan was more likely to touch a coat when asked in the future.

Reinforcers are referred to as being either primary or secondary. *Primary reinforcers* include food, shelter, sleep, and water and are naturally reinforcing; that is, we need them to survive. One way to think of it is that primary reinforcers are things that sustain a new baby's life. *Secondary reinforcers* are *not* reinforcing right after birth, but become reinforcing after being paired frequently with primary reinforcers. That is, a child learns over time that they are "good" things, and therefore he is likely to engage in behaviors to try to get them. For example, the words "Great job!" or "Super!" are not inherently reinforcing, but after a child's parent repeatedly says, "Great job!" paired with other known reinforcers (e.g., hugs and food), the phrase "Great job!" begins to function as a reinforcer. You can use either primary or secondary reinforcers with your child. Keep in mind that if you do use primary reinforcers (e.g., a favorite snack item), pairing them with secondary reinforcers means you can likely fade the primary reinforcers. Then, after your child completes a task, you can reinforce his behavior just by saying, "Great job!" or "Super!" and this will increase the likelihood that your child will engage in that behavior again in the future.

Negative Reinforcement

Negative reinforcement could possibly be one of the most misunderstood terms in our field. As you read this, keep in mind that reinforcement *always* increases a behavior. Now, the *positive* in positive reinforcement just means we are adding (+) something when we provide consequences. Likewise, reinforcement is referred to as negative if we take something away or remove it (-) from the environment (*negative* meaning subtracting) after a behavior and that results in an increase in that behavior.

Here is an example of negative reinforcement. A child has carrots and asparagus on his plate at dinnertime. He is not a big fan of vegetables, but he eats his small serving of carrots. Afterward, his father says, "You ate your carrots so well—you don't have to eat your asparagus," and then removes the asparagus from his son's plate. At the next meal, if the child readily eats his carrots, what kind of reinforcement do you think occurred? If you answered, "Negative reinforcement," you are correct. The *negative* refers to the removal of the asparagus, and we know that reinforcement has occurred if the child eats his carrots the next night (the behavior of eating carrots increases). Now, if the father had wanted to use positive reinforcement in this situation, he might have offered his child a treat such as chocolate for eating his carrots. If the chocolate resulted in the child being more willing to eat his carrots, then it would be positive reinforcement.

The thing to remember is that both negative and positive reinforcement increase behavior. The only difference is that positive reinforcement involves adding something pleasurable to the environment, and negative reinforcement involves removing something that is nonpreferred from the environment. Negative reinforcement happens often as we raise our children.

- A mother can teach her child to ask to remove his coat when he comes in from the cold by immediately taking off his coat when he says, "Off."
- A teacher can increase a student's homework completion by allowing the student to skip homework over the weekend if he completes homework all week long.
- Consider a teenager who has daily chores (e.g., putting his clothes in the hamper, feeding the family pet, and emptying the dishwasher) and weekend chores (e.g., yard cleanup and painting the fence). His mother can use negative reinforcement to increase her son's completion of his daily chores if she reinforces completion of those daily chores by removing one of the weekend chores he dislikes.

In each of these examples, negative reinforcement increases desired behaviors. This means that something the child does not enjoy (e.g., homework or a chore) is removed when the desired behavior occurs. Thus, those desired behaviors will likely increase in the future—*that is negative reinforcement at work!*

We know that this can be a difficult concept to understand, but as you work your way through this chapter and this manual, we will provide additional examples of how negative reinforcement can be used.

Advanced Information → Punishment

Providing a child with reinforcing consequences following appropriate/correct behaviors results in the *increase* of those behaviors. But what can we do about inappropriate or interfering behaviors we want to decrease? When a consequence results in a *decrease* in a behavior, it is referred to as **punishment**. When a child chases the cat and gets swatted, resulting in a scratch, he is less likely to chase the cat again. The swat and resulting scratch are punishers.

Now, often when we hear the word *punishment*, we automatically think of very aversive stimuli such as spanking or yelling. But even a scolding or a reprimand may function as punishment. Those are examples of potential punishment procedures. But, during instruction, we do not need to use these types of punishment procedures.

A natural part of teaching is telling a child when his responses are correct (which hopefully functions as a reinforcer to increase correct responding). But it is also quite natural to tell a child when his response is incorrect. The purpose of telling your child he did something wrong, by saying no or putting an X next to an incorrect problem on a worksheet, is that he will not do it again. If that happens, telling him what was wrong or incorrect is technically punishment.

Some adults will inform a child that he was incorrect by making eye contact, waving a finger, or even using a stern voice. For children with Down syndrome, for whom any social interaction is likely to be a powerful reinforcer, this attempt at punishment may actually *not* decrease incorrect responses. In fact, we often see an *increase* in incorrect responding when caregivers try this. Thus, what was thought to be a punisher actually functions as a reinforcer.

It might be more effective to respond by simply saying, "No" or "Uh uh" in a calm manner without looking directly at the child or even turning your face away from him for a second or two. Then, if the incorrect response decreases, technically these consequences would be considered punishment procedures, because they resulted in a decrease in the preceding behavior.

HANNAH ~ Negative Reinforcement. When Hannah's mother first started teaching Hannah to clean up, she also used negative reinforcement. She said, "You did such a great job cleaning up all the cars—I'll put away all the musical instruments so you don't have to!" Hannah cleaned up more and more!

How to Provide Reinforcement for Correct Responding

When using reinforcement, you must consider what to use as a reinforcer, ensure the child is motivated by that item (i.e., really wants it), and decide how often to give your child the reinforcing item. Let's consider each of these aspects of providing effective reinforcement for correct responses.

Choosing Reinforcers. Remember, a reinforcer is any consequence that follows a behavior and results in an increase in the occurrence of that behavior. There is often confusion between what a child likes, prefers, or enjoys versus what actually increases the occurrence of a desired behavior. You see, even if it seems your child likes or prefers a certain toy, it is only considered a reinforcer if it increases his behavior. For example, one of our daughters really liked different foods, even fruits and vegetables, but bananas (her favorite fruit) did not increase her use of the potty; chocolate did, so it was the reinforcer for using the potty.

A first step to identify potential reinforcers is to think about what items or activities would likely function as reinforcers for your child. Although asking yourself and others is a convenient way to identify reinforcers, it may not be the most effective strategy. Remember, if a child likes something, but it does not increase behavior, it is not a reinforcer. Also, sometimes something will function as a reinforcer in one situation but not another. For example, a teacher said her student loved coloring, because the child continually left her seat to get crayons and then drew in her notebook. But the child's father said he had never seen his daughter color at home, and she even turned away when he asked her to use her crayons. It could be that crayons and coloring are reinforcers, but only at school.

Sometimes something may be misidentified as a reinforcer because it occurs along with the real reinforcer. For example, a speech-language pathologist noted that a toy elephant was an effective reinforcer for a child, but the child's mother shared that her son never seemed interested in this toy at home. It turned out that when the speech-language pathologist gave the child the toy elephant, she sang and played with it, whereas the mother simply handed it to her child when she needed to tend to her other children. In this case, it seems like social interaction was the reinforcer, not the toy elephant.

If you try to teach your child a skill with an item that is not a reinforcer, time and learning opportunities can be lost. Therefore, it might be more efficient to conduct a systematic preference assessment to identify potential reinforcers. This involves systematically presenting your child with one or several items at a time and carefully documenting how he responds. Book 2 provides information about multiple ways to identify potential reinforcers, including by using systematic preference assessments. These systematic procedures may take more time initially, but in the end, may accurately identify reinforcers that enhance your child's learning. Now, remember, just as your preferences change over time, so too do your child's, so you may occasionally need to repeat the preference assessment procedures.

Factors That Influence the Value of Reinforcers. For a consequence to function as a reinforcer, your child must need or want that consequence (i.e., be motivated to get it). One way to increase your child's motivation for something is to limit access to it prior to the teaching session.

JEREMY ~ Factors That Influence the Value of Reinforcers. Jeremy must be motivated to interact with the toys his family is teaching him to reach for and grasp. His family keeps some special toys set aside just for teaching him to reach and grasp. Since he only gets the toys sometimes, he is highly motivated to interact with them when they try to teach him to reach and grasp.

By not giving your child access to a reinforcer, you are creating a state of ***deprivation***, in which the reinforcer (toy) becomes more desirable. Have you ever missed lunch so that by dinnertime you were so hungry you would eat almost anything? Even something that usually is not very appealing (e.g., stale crackers). In this situation, your motivation for food is increased, because you were deprived of food over lunchtime. Alternatively, when a child has *too much* access to a reinforcer, he can enter a state of ***satiation*** and will be less motivated for that reinforcer. No doubt you can imagine a time when you have eaten too much (think about Thanksgiving dinner) and suddenly cannot stand the sight of food. In the first example, the reinforcing value of food has increased, and in the second example, the reinforcing value of food has decreased. These are examples of how events called ***motivating operations*** can change the value of reinforcers. This term makes sense since these events (e.g., missing lunch, Thanksgiving dinner) affect how motivated an individual is to obtain a specific item.

JEREMY ~ Satiation. Jeremy's parents accidentally left the special toys out after teaching their son to reach and grasp. When they went to teach Jeremy to reach and grasp the next day, they realized he had been looking at the toys that morning. By the time they began instruction, he had lost interest; he hardly looked at the toys and did not even reach. Jeremy was not motivated to interact with the toys, because he had already seen the toys. They made sure to put the toys away each day.

How Often Should You Provide a Reinforcer? How often a reinforcer is provided is referred to as the ***schedule of reinforcement.*** We know that when reinforcement follows a behavior, that behavior increases. So, at the beginning of instruction, it is critical to provide reinforcement after *every* correct response, to increase correct responding. This is described in terms of a ratio of 1 response to 1 reinforcer; for every one response, the child receives one reinforcer. The technical way to describe this is a ***fixed ratio 1*** or ***FR1*** schedule of reinforcement (also called a ***continuous schedule of reinforcement).*** The word *ratio* refers to the fact that a certain number of responses are required and the word *fixed* refers to the fact that the same number of responses is required to receive reinforcement each time.

As your child begins to respond correctly during instruction, any additional reinforcers (such as a sticker or treat) should be faded, similar to fading prompts. This is important in helping your child perform skills without immediately receiving some extra or additional reinforcer every time he performs the skill. This will also help to maintain your child's skills over time.

We can still describe this in terms of a ratio; in this case, for every [insert number] of responses, the child receives a reinforcer, where the number could be two, three, or even more. Thus, the schedule of reinforcement has changed from an FR1 to an FR2 or FR3, etc. These schedules provide reinforcers more intermittently and are referred to as ***intermittent schedules of reinforcement.*** Changing the schedule of reinforcement from a continuous to intermittent schedule is called ***thinning the schedule of reinforcement*** or ***fading reinforcement.***

HANNAH ~ Thinning the Schedule of Reinforcement. When Hannah's mother first taught Hannah to clean up, she provided reinforcement (positive reinforcement in the form of praise and access to her iPad for a few minutes and negative reinforcement in the form of tidying up some toys for her). But Hannah's mother really wanted Hannah to clean up without needing to give her the iPad each time. It was getting difficult to juggle the need to clean up before leaving the house for school or errands and allowing Hannah to play with the iPad for five minutes. So Hannah's mother began to give Hannah access to the iPad only after every few times she cleaned up. Eventually her mother let Hannah play on the iPad at the end of the day if she had cleaned up when asked over the course of the day. Over time, cleaning up became part of Hannah's daily routine, and her mother completely faded giving Hannah the iPad as a consequence for cleaning up.

Keep in mind, there are reinforcers that should be faded and then there are natural reinforcers for engaging in a behavior that should not be faded. Playing on the iPad every time Hannah cleaned up was not a natural consequence related to cleaning up (though a neat and tidy room in which she could find all of her toys was). But praise, which is a natural consequence for many behaviors, may not be something you want to fade entirely.

As you thin or fade reinforcement, one way to build in time between your child's correct responses and access to reinforcement is to use a ***token reinforcement system*** (also referred to as a ***token economy***). With a token system, the child receives a token (a sticker, check mark, etc.) for each correct response and then, after making the required number of responses, receives the reinforcer. To use a token system with Hannah, her mother delayed giving her the iPad by checking off each time she cleaned up throughout the day. When she accumulated four check marks, her mother gave her the iPad. The reinforcer the child receives for earning a specified number of tokens is referred to as the ***backup reinforcer***. A token system is a great visual support to use as you fade reinforcement. We discuss how to set up a token system in Book 2, Chapter 4.

Advanced Information → Schedules of Reinforcement

We already described fixed ratio schedules of reinforcement, one of the basic schedules of reinforcement. There are, in fact, four basic schedules of reinforcement: fixed ratio, variable ratio, fixed interval, and variable interval. Remember, with a *fixed* ratio schedule, reinforcement is provided after a certain number of responses (the ratio part), and that ratio remains constant (the fixed part). With a ratio schedule, the more quickly your child responds, the sooner he will receive reinforcement.

With an interval schedule of reinforcement, how many times your child responds does not matter; what matters is the passage of some interval of time, and then the next response results in reinforcement. For example, a child receives a token following the first time he remains in the shopping cart after a three-minute interval; this is a fixed interval schedule of three minutes. The term *fixed* means that the number of responses required before reinforcement remains the same (ratio) or the amount of time remains the same (interval); that is, it is fixed. The schedule is noted as FR followed by the number of responses for fixed ratio (e.g., FR2, FR3, etc.) or FI followed by the duration of the interval for fixed interval (e.g., FI3, FI5, etc.).

Ratio and interval schedules can be either fixed, as we have described thus far, or variable. In variable schedules, the variable part means that the number of responses or interval of time varies. In this case, the schedule is noted in the same way fixed schedules are noted, but the number refers to the *average* number of responses or average interval of time required for reinforcement (e.g., VR2, VR4, etc., or VI2, VI6, etc.). For example, a variable ratio schedule 3 (VR3) would mean that, on average, every third response results in reinforcement; the child could make two responses and receive reinforcement, then four responses and receive reinforcement, and then three more responses and receive reinforcement, averaging out to every three responses (i.e., 2+4+3=9; 9/3=3).

The variable aspect is systematic and planned rather than by chance. To use a variable schedule requires preplanning in which you identify the maximum number of responses or time interval for the schedule and refer to an online random number generator to identify the specific numbers of responses or time intervals (e.g., http://randomnumber-generator.intemodino.com/en/ or https://www.randomizer.org/).

What is interesting about these different schedules of reinforcement is that we respond differently depending on the type of schedule and size of the ratio or interval. Overall, your child will tend to respond more consistently without any pauses in responding with variable schedules (both ratio and interval).

HELPFUL HINT　**Tips for Providing Reinforcers**
- **Provide the reinforcer immediately after the desired behavior.** *Immediate* means less than one second to at most a few seconds after the behavior occurs. Any longer and the behavior you are trying to increase is less likely to increase. This is because other behaviors may occur between the target behavior and the reinforcer. Then, the behavior that occurred just before you gave your child the reinforcer will likely increase, not the target behavior that you want to increase. Sometimes this means that a behavior you would prefer your child not do, such as out-of-seat behavior in school or playing with his food at dinner, is followed by reinforcement and that behavior will be the one that increases.
- **Provide small amounts of a reinforcer.** To prevent satiation, provide only a small amount of the reinforcer at a time. This may mean giving a small amount of a primary reinforcer (food or drink). If you are providing access to secondary reinforcers (a toy or preferred activity), this means providing access for only a few moments. A great way to let your child

know when time with a reinforcer is up is by using a timer. You can set the time (on your smartphone, the stove, an egg timer, or portable digital timer), and then when it goes off, draw your child's attention to it and remove the reinforcer (e.g., the toy). Using a token system can also prevent satiation, as your child does not access the reinforcer until he responds correctly several times.

- **Use social attention as a reinforcer.** As we keep mentioning, social interest is a strength for many children with Down syndrome, so your child will likely find social attention to be a particularly powerful reinforcer. **Social attention** includes

  - social praise such as saying, "Great job!" or "You did it!"

  - physical interaction such as hugs and tickles

  - play interactions such as building with blocks after the child requests blocks or having a conversation about a fun trip to the park when the child initiates a conversation

  You can also pair any other reinforcer with social attention. You can even make things that might not be so reinforcing more reinforcing by making them social. Playing the "drums" on an overturned pot in a band with Mom or stacking plastic containers by taking turns with Dad and watching them fall can make ordinary household items reinforcing. Also, a favorite activity that does not involve an actual item may be reinforcing (e.g., bouncing your child on your knee, singing a favorite song or finger play such as the "Itsy Bitsy Spider," or telling knock-knock jokes).

- **Provide behavior-specific praise.** *Behavior-specific praise* includes a description of the behavior the child performed paired with praise. For example, after your child cleans up her toys, say, "Thank you! You did a great job cleaning up your toys!" or, after your child gets his shoes, say, "I love the way you found your shoes!" This lets your child know exactly what he did that was great!

- **Reinforce prompted and independent responses.** At the beginning of instruction, be sure to reinforce correct responses, even if prompted. When your child begins to perform the skill independently, provide even more or higher quality reinforcement for independent responses than prompted responses. This is called **differential reinforcement,** something we discuss later in this chapter.

- **Set up a contingency.** It is important to be consistent about allowing your child access to certain reinforcers used during instruction. You can choose some reinforcers that are only provided **contingent** on the correct response. This means that, if your child is supposed to practice requesting his coloring book and crayons, he should **only** be given those items when he requests them correctly.

- **Use visuals to represent reinforcers that your child can choose.** Giving your child an opportunity to choose the reinforcers he can receive will likely increase their effectiveness. Cut out pictures to illustrate the reinforcers, even for activity reinforcers (e.g., a spider for the "Itsy Bitsy Spider" song) and allow your child to choose from the array of pictures.

HELPFUL HINT   **Steps for Using Negative Reinforcement**

1. **Identify situations that your child may want to have come to an end.** For example, when is he usually ready to get out of his high chair, crib, or car seat?

2. **Once your child makes the correct response, immediately get him out of the situation.** For example, you can prompt your child to say or sign "Down," and reinforce that response by taking him out of his high chair; you can prompt him to say or sign "Up," and reinforce that response by taking him out of his crib; and you can prompt him to say or sign "Out," and reinforce that response by taking him out of his car seat.

3. **Provide behavior-specific praise.** You can also provide behavior-specific praise when using negative reinforcement. For example, as soon as her child said "Down," one mother took him out of the high chair and provided behavior-specific praise: "What a big boy! You said 'Down' when you wanted to get out of your high chair! That was great!"

What to Do When Your Child Makes an Incorrect Response

The goal of instruction is to make sure your child makes as many correct responses as possible, so that each can be followed by a reinforcing consequence. Then, those correct responses will increase. We use prompts to enhance correct responding, but sometimes your child will make an incorrect response *with* or *without* a prompt. On some occasions, you may be able to prevent your child from responding incorrectly. This is called *response interruption*. For example, while teaching shapes, colors, or letters, you may see your child moving his hand to touch the wrong shape, color, or letter; you can then merely guide his hand to the correct response. But, you cannot easily interrupt all types of incorrect responses. For example, it is difficult to prevent a child from *saying* an incorrect answer.

When you are developing your child's programs, you will decide what to do when he makes an error.

- First, decide how you will respond to the incorrect response.
  - ➤ Be sure *not* to respond to an incorrect response with reinforcement, because that will result in an increase in incorrect responding. Some interventionists respond to an incorrect response with endearing words of encouragement such as "That was good trying sweetie—try again." This type of verbal interaction, paired with eye contact and physical interaction (e.g., a pat on the back, tap on the arm), is social attention. We know this can be very reinforcing, and the child may learn, "If I want all of that attention from my mom/teacher, I can make any response and get it."
  - ➤ Consider removing social attention following an incorrect response to decrease the likelihood of that behavior occurring in the future. See **Advanced Information ➡ A Strategy to Decrease Incorrect Responding** for a discussion of the effectiveness of this approach. You can remove attention by merely turning your face away from the child while remaining silent for a second or two. We have found this to be very effective for young children with Down syndrome, as you are not only decreasing future incorrect responses, but you may also be increasing your child's motivation to respond correctly in order to get your attention on the next learning opportunity.
  - ➤ You may also consider providing feedback such as saying, "Uh uh," "Try again," or "No," to let your child know he did not give the correct response.
- Then, decide how you will respond during the next opportunity.
  - ➤ You can present another S^D and then use a more intrusive prompt than the prompt you used when your child made an error. Or you can introduce a prompt if you did not provide one. By introducing a more intrusive prompt, you can be fairly certain your child will respond correctly. You may want to do this several times in a row; this is called ***massed practice***.
  - ➤ You can present another opportunity in the same way. Your child *may* respond correctly on that next opportunity or may continue to make incorrect responses. If your child makes another error, it makes sense to then introduce a more intrusive prompt on the subsequent opportunity. The goal is to prevent errors from occurring.

MEGAN ~ Consequences Following Incorrect Responses. After Megan learned to pick up the coat when asked, her teacher and parents checked every so often to make sure she continued to do so correctly. At times, Megan picked up a different item when her teacher asked her for the coat. When this happened, her teacher decided to respond by looking away briefly and removing the items to end the learning opportunity. This was recorded as an incorrect response. Then, after a few seconds, she placed the items out again and asked Megan to pick the coat. To ensure that Megan responded correctly this time, she immediately used the least intrusive prompt, pointing at the coat from six inches away. When Megan responded correctly on this learning opportunity, her teacher noted that she responded with a prompt.

Advanced Information → A Strategy to Decrease Incorrect Responding

You may question the idea of withholding social attention after your child responds incorrectly. But, this can be a very powerful way to respond to incorrect responses and is consistent with what we know about the Down syndrome behavioral phenotype. For most children with Down syndrome, social consequences function as powerful reinforcers and can be used to teach a wide range of skills. Any social attention you provide following your child's response (correct or incorrect) is likely to function as a reinforcer and increase that response in the future. But we want to increase correct responding, not incorrect responding. This means you should provide social attention following a correct response, but not after an incorrect response.

Some take this a step further and very clearly remove the opportunity for social attention following incorrect responses. In this case, you provide social attention following correct responses but block social attention following incorrect responses. For example, you might block attention by turning away and not talking to your child. Withholding social attention following incorrect responses has been demonstrated to decrease incorrect responding and increase correct responding. One group of researchers (Drash, Raver, Murrin, and Tudor, 1989) even showed how effective this was specifically with children with Down syndrome who were learning to imitate sounds and words.

What to Do When Your Child Does Not Respond at All

Sometimes your child will make an incorrect response (e.g., when Megan touched the pants instead of the coat), but other times, your child will not respond at all to the S^D. This is an error too. For example, you may ask your child, "Where's the coat?" and she may not respond in any way.

If you are using a time delay prompt fading procedure and your child does not respond within the time delay, you should prompt him. If you are not using a time delay and your child does not respond to the S^D, you can respond as though it were an error, as described previously. If your child continues not to respond on the next opportunity or two, try asking him to do something that you know is within his repertoire (e.g., ask for a "high five" or to point to a body part). Then, present the original S^D again. Most importantly, do not give your child lots of social attention when he does not respond. Some caregivers may begin to coax the child (e.g., "Please let me see you do it. Please."). When they do this, they are responding to an incorrect response with social attention, and you know what will happen then, right? The child's refusals to respond will likely increase.

If your child continues not to respond at all, and you are confident that an illness or other physical cause is not the reason, you may want to reexamine your instruction. Ask yourself:

- Was my child attending to the S^D? Sometimes children are not paying attention and miss the opportunity to respond. Be sure you get your child's attention prior to presenting an S^D. We discuss this in more detail in Book 2, Chapter 3.
- Does the prompt result in my child responding correctly? If not, then it is not an effective prompt for your child. Consider using a more intrusive prompt (i.e., one that provides more assistance and thus ensures the correct response will occur) or a different type of prompt.
- Is the planned consequence truly reinforcing? It may not be. Even if it was reinforcing in the past, several factors can influence the effectiveness of a reinforcer. See Book 2, Chapters 3 and 4, for more information on choosing reinforcers.
- Is it reinforcing for my child *not* to respond? If you interact with your child while he is not responding, you could be positively reinforcing lack of responding to the S^D. Alternatively, if you end instruction just after he stops responding, not responding may be negatively reinforced (i.e., you removed the demands to respond, in which case refusals to respond will increase). We suggest you use similar consequences as you do for an incorrect response—that is, withhold social attention for a few seconds and then present another learning opportunity (deliver the

S^D again)— but this time, make sure to use a prompt that results in the correct response and then provide a reinforcer.

What if you answered yes to all the questions above, but your child still *consistently* does not respond during instruction? When your child consistently does not respond at all during instruction, he is engaging in noncompliance. There are several strategies you can use to address noncompliance; these are actually the same strategies we discuss in the section on behavior that interferes with learning at the end of this chapter and in more detail in Book 2, Chapters 2–5.

Planning Each of Your Child's Instructional Programs

For each specific skill you want to teach your child, writing down how you will implement the strategies will help you plan for instruction. We provide a **Program Planner** to help you do this. Planning and writing out the steps for each skill you want to teach increases the likelihood you will consistently use the strategies you have just learned. It is also one way you can share strategies for each program with teachers or other caregivers who might also be teaching your child. In addition to the strategies in this chapter, be sure to refer to the information for each teaching program in Book 2 as you plan, especially when you first get started! You will see as you read through Book 2, Chapters 2–5, that there are decisions to make about how to teach each skill. We provide ideas about prompting each skill, pairing social attention with other reinforcement, and error correction procedures. But, each of these components of instruction must be individualized to your child. As you begin instruction and figure out what works, the same prompts, reinforcers, and error correction procedures are likely to be effective for many of the skills you teach your child.

JEREMY ~ Planning Your Child's Instructional Programs. The first thing Jeremy's family did when they wanted to start teaching him to reach for and grasp toys was to plan how they would do it. This was really important because Jeremy's parents would be teaching Jeremy at home, but Jeremy also spent some days with his grandparents, who would teach Jeremy at their house. Everyone needed to be sure they were doing the same thing to help Jeremy learn. They used a program planner to document how they were going to teach reaching and grasping.

As you can see on the Program Planner (next page), there are spaces to record prompting, reinforcement, and error correction procedures. There are also a few more decisions to make about how to teach each skill. On the Program Planner, you will be asked to decide the context in which you will teach—where, when, and how often you will teach each skill as well as probing for maintenance. You will also

Program Planner

Name: Jeremy   **Program:** Manipulating Objects: Reach and
Palmar Grasp

(Discrete trial teaching)   **Instruction embedded within an activity**   **Naturalistic instruction**

Materials: small lightweight toys—rattle, musical toy, plush ducky

S^D: place an object within Jeremy's reach and make sure he is looking at the object by shaking or activating it

Target Skill: reach and grasp = Jeremy will reach for the object by raising and moving one or both arms toward an object and wrap his hand(s) around the object, lifting it off the surface

Prompt: physical guidance

Consequences:
   Correct response—if Jeremy reaches for the object, immediately (within 1 second) provide social attention, including verbal praise (e.g., "Wow! Nice reaching for the object!") and play with the object with Jeremy for a few seconds
   Incorrect response—if Jeremy engages in a different response than reaching, do not look directly at him or say anything, end the opportunity, wait 2 to 3 seconds, and then present another opportunity
   No response—if Jeremy does not respond to a partial prompt or by the end of the 5-second time delay, provide a more intrusive prompt

Prompt Fading: (most-to-least prompt fading with a time delay)
   Full prompt (FP) = immediately place your hand on Jeremy's hand and guide him to reach for and grasp the object
   Partial prompt (PP) = gently tap Jeremy's elbow to guide him to reach and grasp
   Time delay = wait 5 seconds to allow Jeremy to independently reach and grasp

Planning for Generalization: Mom, Dad, Grandma, and Grandpa will present opportunities in all different rooms in each of their houses and use different types of toys (see Materials)

Criterion for Mastery: 80% or better correct responding across two consecutive sessions, two days, and two caregivers

Probing for Maintenance: as Jeremy plays with toys throughout the day, practice every day and probe, recording his/her continued progress, once per week

decide how you will keep track of your child's progress so you know he is learning. Let's consider each of these next.

Tracking Your Child's Progress

How do you know if your child is learning all the skills you are teaching? You might think you can just remember his performance for each skill. But, just take a moment to flip through Book 2 to see how many skills you will be teaching. It is much more useful to record your child's performance as you teach. That means writing down what your child does. Do not worry; you do not have to note performance every time you teach (although some families and professionals may choose to do that). You may choose to note your child's progress just once or twice per week. We will show you several ways of recording your child's performance so you can choose what works best for your family (see Appendix A and Book 2).

Recording your child's performance will help you do the following:
- determine when or if you need to change a prompt to improve performance;
- determine when to fade the prompt so your child learns to respond independently;
- monitor changes or patterns in your child's behavior (e.g., behavior to gain attention or to try to get out of the instructional situation; better performance with one caregiver versus another);
- determine whether your child could benefit from more learning opportunities;
- remind all your child's caregivers to actually present learning opportunities;
- monitor the skills your child has acquired and those still in need of intervention; and
- prepare for meetings in which decisions regarding your child's services will be made (at annual meetings or as your child transitions from early intervention to preschool services or from preschool services to kindergarten).

Tracking your child's progress can be very reinforcing for your teaching behavior—which means you will keep teaching!

Progress trackers (also referred to as datasheets, progress monitoring forms, and tracking forms) can help you record your child's performance and provide a summary of his progress. A progress tracker offers an easy and concise way to record how your child performs. In Book 2 we discuss putting together a binder to keep track of your child's programs and progress. We include templates for the progress trackers and other forms in the appendix to Book 2.

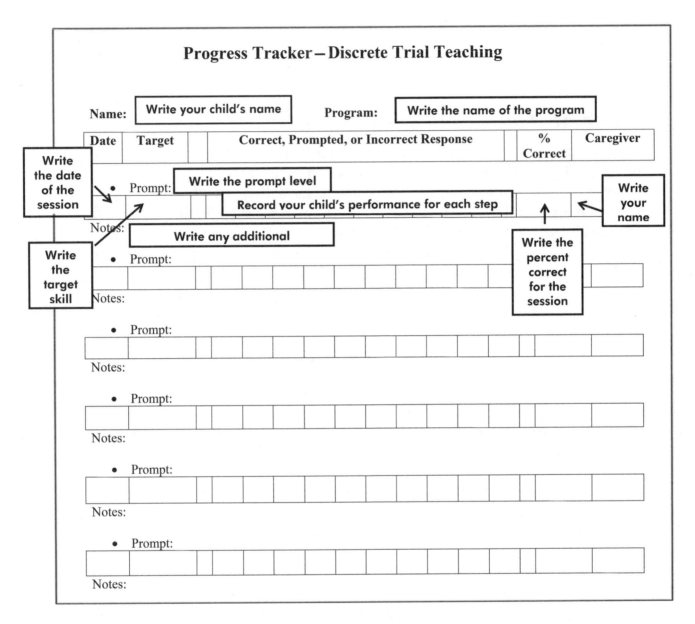

Progress Tracker—Discrete Trial Teaching

Name: Write your child's name   **Program:** Write the name of the program

Write the date of the session

Write the target skill

Prompt: Write the prompt level

Record your child's performance for each step

Write any additional

Write the percent correct for the session

Write your name

Date	Target		Correct, Prompted, or Incorrect Response		% Correct	Caregiver

Each row of boxes on the progress tracker refers to a session, and each box refers to a learning opportunity. You will begin each session by recording the date, current target skill, current prompt level, and the initials of the person implementing intervention that session. During the session, record performance on each opportunity, and at the end, calculate a summary percentage of correct responding.

JEREMY ~ Progress Tracker. Jeremy's caregivers tracked his progress learning to reach and grasp. On the Progress Tracker, they recorded the prompt level and Jeremy's performance for each opportunity each session. They used a most-to-least prompt fading procedure with a time delay, fading from a full to a partial prompt and then introducing a time delay.

Progress Tracker — Discrete Trial Teaching

Name: *Jeremy*   **Program:** *Manipulating Objects: Reach and Palmar Grasp*

Date	Target	Correct, Prompted, or Incorrect Response									% Correct	Caregiver

Prompt: *Full prompt*

| 12/4 | Reach and palmar grasp | FP | - | FP | FP | FP | FP | FP | FP | FP | FP | 90% | Mom |

Notes: *the - occurred when he threw his hands up in the air and did not respond at all*

Prompt: *Full prompt*

| 12/5 | Reach and palmar grasp | FP | FP | FP | FP | FP | - | FP | FP | FP | FP | 90% | Grandma |

Notes: *same behavior for the one -*

Prompt: *Partial prompt*

| 12/6 | Reach and palmar grasp | PP | PP | FP | PP | PP | PP | PP | - | PP | PP | 80% | Mom |

Notes: *same behavior for the -*

Prompt: *Partial prompt*

| 12/7 | Reach and palmar grasp | PP | PP | PP | PP | - | PP | PP | PP | PP | PP | 90% | Grandma |

Notes: *just one - for throwing his hands up and turning away*

Prompt: *Time delay*

| 12/8 | Reach and palmar grasp | + | + | - | + | + | + | PP | + | PP | + | 70% | Mom |

Notes:

Prompt: *Time delay*

| 12/10 | Reach and palmar grasp | + | + | + | PP | + | + | PP | + | + | + | 80% | Grandma |

Notes:

Record Performance on Each Opportunity

On your progress tracker, when you record your child's performance on each learning opportunity, in each box record one of the following:

- a plus sign (+) for a correct response (we use a + to indicate independent responding, that is, responding without presenting a prompt).
- a minus sign (-) for an incorrect response (you can also record *NR* for *no response*).
- the level of prompt such as *FP* (*full prompt*/most intrusive prompt) and *PP* (*partial prompt*/less intrusive or minimal prompt). Alternatively, some caregivers may note the type of prompt (e.g., VP for verbal prompt or GP for gestural prompt).

Calculate Summary Percentage of Correct Responses during Each Session

Looking at each row/session during which you recorded performance, the summary percentage of correct responses during each session is shown in the second-to-last box. Use the following formula to calculate the percentage of correct responses during each session:

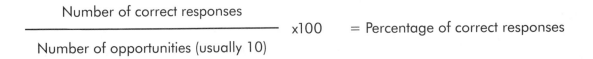

$$\frac{\text{Number of correct responses}}{\text{Number of opportunities (usually 10)}} \times 100 = \text{Percentage of correct responses}$$

What counts as a correct response depends on the prompt level; that is why it is so important to note the prompt level on the Progress Tracker. If you are at a full prompt level, then any correct responses your child makes following a full prompt and any completely independent responses are correct responses. This allows you to see how your child is responding to the full prompt. Either the prompt is working and he is responding correctly on most opportunities, or it is not, in which case, consider changing the prompt. Remember, we said that usually we set criteria for deciding whether a child is performing successfully and we can fade a prompt at 80 percent or more correct responding across two sessions, sometimes also two days and even two caregivers.

JEREMY ~ Calculate Percentage of Correct Responses with Full Prompt. Jeremy's caregivers recorded his performance on each opportunity. They started with a full prompt. After only two sessions, Jeremy responded correctly following the full prompt on all but one opportunity (recorded as a -) each session, scoring 90 percent correct for each session.

If you are at a partial prompt level, then any correct responses your child makes following the partial prompt and any completely independent responses) are correct responses. If you must reintroduce a full prompt on any opportunity, record that you did so, but it is considered an *incorrect* response when calculating your child's summary percentage of correct responses. His response is incorrect at this point because you want him to be responding to a partial prompt. This way of counting correct and incorrect responses allows you to see how your child is responding to the partial prompt. Either the partial prompt is working, and he is responding correctly on most opportunities, or it is not, in which case, you want to consider changing the prompt. See sessions 12/6 and 12/7 of performance recording on Jeremy's Progress Tracker for examples of calculating summary percentage of correct responses.

JEREMY ~ Calculate Percentage of Correct Responses with Partial Prompt. After Jeremy completed two sessions at or above 80 percent with a full prompt, his parents faded the prompt. During the next two sessions (on 12/6 and 12/7), they used a partial prompt and Jeremy again responded very well. Note that in each session, he did not respond correctly on one opportunity; in fact, he just threw his hands in the air and turned away, so his caregivers recorded a minus for those opportunities. He also did not respond to the partial prompt on one opportunity in the first partial prompt session, and his caregivers needed to reintroduce a full prompt (recorded as FP). He correctly responded to the PP 8 times out of 10 total opportunities in the first session and 9 times out of 10 total opportunities in the second session. He scored 80 and 90 percent correct responding, respectively.

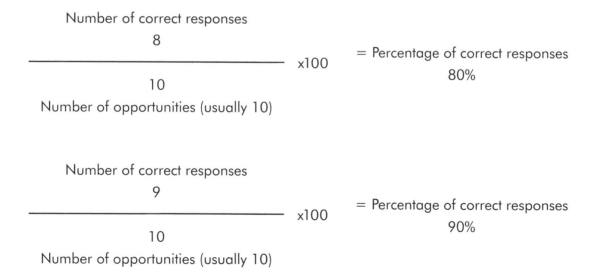

If you have introduced a time delay, you want your child to be responding before the end of the delay interval and before you deliver the prompt, that is, responding **independently**. Data collection at this level will be a bit different. Now, any correct response before the end of the delay is recorded as a plus sign (+) and is considered a correct independent response. If your child does not respond by the end of the delay and you introduce a prompt (recording a PP or FP), this would now *not* be counted as a correct response when summarizing performance. And of course, if your child responded incorrectly and you recorded a minus sign (-), it would also not be counted as a correct response when summarizing performance.

This way of counting correct independent and other responses allows you to see how your child is responding independently. It is *independent* performance we are interested in during time delay and when deciding if a child has mastered a skill. **Mastery** criterion is usually set similarly to our criteria for deciding if a child is successfully responding to a prompt, but now, we are only counting independent correct responses. So, mastery criterion is usually something like 80 percent or better (depending on the skill) *independent* correct responses across two consecutive sessions and sometimes also two days and two caregivers. Two sessions, days, and caregivers help ensure your child continues to respond correctly, not just once.

JEREMY ~ Calculate Percentage of Correct Responses during Time Delay Sessions. When his caregivers began time delay in the next session (12/8), Jeremy responded fairly well. He responded independently (indicated by +) on seven opportunities in the first time delay session. On two opportunities his caregivers provided a partial prompt, because he had not reached or grasped at the end of the time delay. Again, on one opportunity he did not respond correctly at all, instead throwing his hands in the air and turning away. Because this was time delay, only the responses marked with + count as correct responses. This way Jeremy's caregivers can see if he is reaching and grasping all on his own.

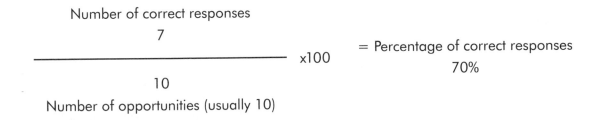

$$\frac{\underset{7}{\overset{\text{Number of correct responses}}{\rule{0pt}{0pt}}}}{\underset{\text{Number of opportunities (usually 10)}}{10}} \times 100 = \begin{array}{c}\text{Percentage of correct responses}\\ 70\%\end{array}$$

Jeremy did well on the next time delay session (12/10), scoring an 80 percent (he needed a partial prompt on only two opportunities when he did not reach and grasp the toy at the end of the time delay). At this point he had not yet met mastery criteria for independently reaching and grasping, though he was well on his way. Jeremy's family conducted more sessions until he reached independent performance at or above 80 percent across two consecutive sessions across two days and two caregivers, indicating Jeremy had mastered this skill.

As you record your child's progress on the Progress Tracker with a summary of correct responses, it will be helpful to graph his summary performance on a **Graph** so you can see how it changes over time and make adjustments to instruction if needed. For each session, you will write in the date on the horizontal axis and put a dot (called a ***data point***) at the corresponding level of performance (shown on the vertical axis). Next you will connect data points with a straight line (called a ***data path***). It is helpful to label the prompt level and separate prompt levels by drawing a vertical line. You can even indicate when your child has mastered a skill by noting a star above the data point.

Graph

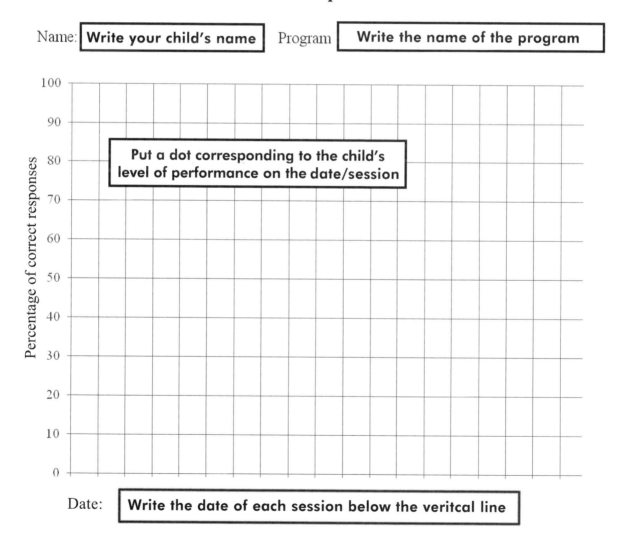

Name: | Write your child's name | Program | Write the name of the program

Percentage of correct responses

Put a dot corresponding to the child's level of performance on the date/session

Date: | **Write the date of each session below the veritcal line**

JEREMY ~ Graph Your Child's Progress. Jeremy's caregivers used a graph to visually depict his progress learning to reach and grasp. Each session they transferred his summary percentage correct responses to the graph, making sure to note when they had changed a prompt. The graph helped them see that Jeremy was making great progress learning to reach and grasp.

Graph

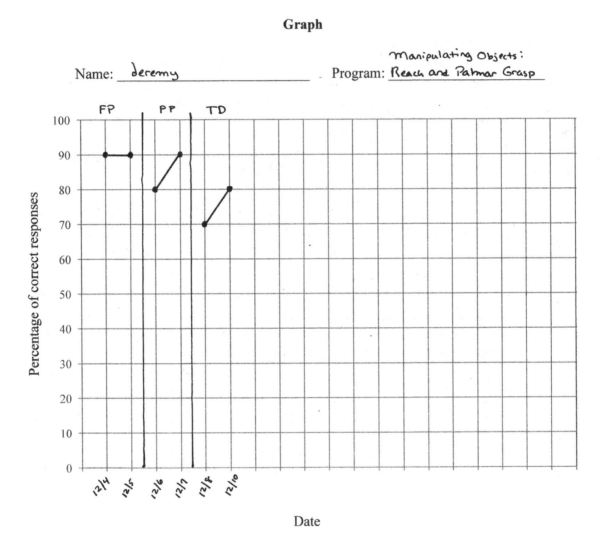

Name: _Jeremy_

Program: _Manipulating Objects: Reach and Palmar Grasp_

Date

Where, When, and How Often to Teach New Skills: Contexts for Instruction

By now you probably have an idea of the prompting, reinforcement, and error correction procedures to use when teaching your child a specific skill, as well as how to write the Program Plan and record progress. Now let's consider where, when, and how often you want to teach a particular skill. There are many different ways to create opportunities to teach your child all of the skills he needs to learn to meet his potential.

When teaching skills, Jeremy's, Megan's, and Hannah's caregivers all used the same principles and procedures you have been reading about. But their instruction varied in intensity in terms of the number of learning opportunities presented, as well as where instruction occurred, with whom, when, and for how long. These variables, taken together, make up the *context of instruction*.

JEREMY ~ Contexts for Instruction. When Jeremy's parents and grandparents taught him to reach and grasp, they did so by providing many opportunities during several sessions each day. This included while he was playing in his crib and on the living room floor with his toys.

MEGAN ~ Contexts for Instruction. Megan's mother and teacher taught Megan to identify coats while Megan played with her dolls, one of her favorite activities. They could easily embed several opportunities for her to retrieve a coat for each doll as they played dress-up, getting ready for school, etc. with the dolls.

HANNAH ~ Contexts for Instruction. When Hannah's mother taught her to clean up, she did so during the routine opportunities that naturally arose each day to clean up. This included when leaving for school and before bedtime.

The next sections describe three contexts that can be used when teaching the skills in this manual to children with Down syndrome. We included examples about teaching counting to illustrate the application of instruction for the same skill across three different contexts.

Discrete Trial Teaching

When Jeremy's parents and grandparents presented many teaching opportunities several times a day to teach reach and grasp, they were implementing *discrete trial teaching* (also referred to as *explicit instruction, discrete trial instruction,* and *massed trial instruction*), which is a caregiver-directed context for instruction. The caregiver provides several learning opportunities in a row, prompting correct responses, and providing individually tailored reinforcers for correct responses. Many opportunities are provided to practice one target skill (e.g., counting three objects, receptively identifying a coat) in one session before then teaching another skill and presenting many opportunities for that skill in a session. Typically, discrete trial teaching takes place with only one child; however, it can be used in small groups with two to three children at a time.

To illustrate how this method might be used to teach a child to count three objects, a mother may place three objects in front of him and ask, "How many are there?" She then models pointing and saying each number, providing a reinforcer after her child responds correctly. As soon as the child finishes the reinforcer (i.e., consumes a food/drink or plays with a toy), his mother presents another opportunity, continuing this way for several opportunities.

You may have noticed that the progress tracker described previously was called **Progress Tracker – Discrete Trial Teaching**. The tracker works well in discrete trial instruction, as it is set up to record a child's performance on multiple repeated opportunities of the same target skill with a different page for each target skill.

Instruction Embedded within an Activity

When Megan's mother and teacher taught her to identify coats while playing with dolls, they were implementing *instruction embedded within an activity*, which is also referred to as *activity-based instruction* or *activity-based intervention* (Pretti-Frontczak & Bricker, 2004). When teaching within this context, you engage your child in a specific activity and then embed learning opportunities within the activity. The activity should allow for several opportunities to practice several target skills. As with any instruction, caregivers prompt correct responses and provide reinforcement, but generally the activity itself provides reinforcement (e.g., once the child has put the train tracks together, practicing fine motor skills, he can play with the trains).

To illustrate, a parent may play the game Connect 4 with her child who is learning to count. During the course of the game, the child can practice counting skills along with other skills such as identifying colors and picking up small pieces (fine motor skills). The consequences for counting and other correct responses are embedded within the game—continuing to play the game.

Progress Tracker – Instruction Embedded within an Activity

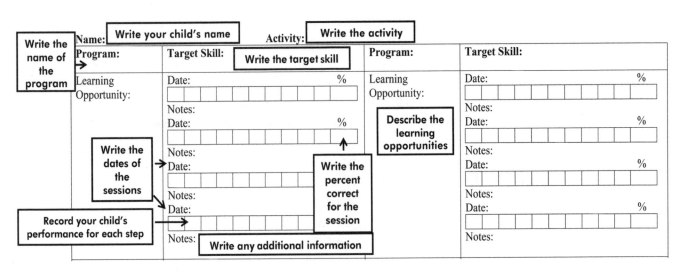

To keep track of your child's progress during this type of instruction, we suggest using the **Progress Tracker – Instruction Embedded within an Activity**. Record one activity on each page, keeping track of several different skills you will address within that particular activity. The list of skills also functions as a prompt for you to ensure you address each skill a few times.

Naturalistic Instruction

When teaching cleanup within routine opportunities, Hannah's mother was using *naturalistic instruction,* which is also referred to as *milieu teaching* and *incidental teaching*. In general, naturalistic instruction means that, while you engage your child in everyday activities, you take advantage of naturally occurring learning opportunities to prompt and reinforce target skills.

To illustrate, while making dinner one night, a father needed three pots. He took out three pots and asked his son, to count them. Because his son was just learning to count, his father prompted him by modeling pointing to each pot and saying, "One, two, three." The natural consequence for counting in this situation was getting a big thank-you for helping. Sometimes, caregivers direct opportunities, such as asking a child to count the pots. But, opportunities are often child initiated. For example, you might take advantage of your child's interest in the frozen peas you are preparing for dinner. You could give your child a small number to put in the bowl to be heated in the microwave and then prompt him to count each.

Progress Tracker – Naturalistic Instruction

Naturalistic instruction involves opportunities spread out over time and mixed with opportunities to practice other skills. During dinner preparation, the caregiver presents opportunities for the child to count as well as name his colors, request food items, and speak in two-word utterances. Later in the evening, as the child is taking out books to read at bedtime, his father asks him to count the books, read a few sight words, and practice clearly articulating words. You see how the opportunities to practice any given skill (e.g., counting) are spread out throughout the day and mixed in with opportunities to practice many other skills.

To track your child's progress during naturalistic instruction, you might record your child's progress on a progress tracker that allows you to record a few different skills during naturalistic learning opportunities that occur throughout your child's day. We suggest using something like the **Progress Tracker – Naturalistic Instruction** on the previous page.

Choosing a Context for Instruction

How do you decide which of these three contexts to use when teaching your child with Down syndrome any given skill? The answer depends on the intensity of instruction needed.

These contexts exist along a continuum of the intensity of instruction.
- The number of opportunities varies from a few (naturalistic instruction) to many (discrete trial teaching).
- The spacing of the opportunities varies from long times between learning opportunities (naturalistic instruction) to very short times (discrete trial teaching).
- Often the type of consequence varies from natural reinforcers (naturalistic instruction) to child-specific reinforcers (discrete trial instruction).
- The number of children present who are also receiving instruction varies from many (naturalistic instruction) to one or maybe two (discrete trial teaching).

This continuum has room for lots of variation. For example, when using naturalistic instruction embedded with an activity, you can present several opportunities in a row to practice a skill. You can also use other reinforcers as consequences within these contexts (e.g., provide a piece of pretzel for counting correctly).

There are a number of factors to consider in choosing the context or intensity with which to provide instruction:
- What are your child's strengths and weaknesses?
    - Weaknesses are likely to make some skills more difficult for your child to learn, and those skills may warrant a more intense intervention such as discrete trial teaching.

- ➤ In contrast, skills involving areas of strength such as your child's special interests or phenotypic strengths may be easy to learn with less intensive intervention such as naturalistic instruction.
- We have found that a faster pace—that is, shorter spacing such as several seconds between opportunities—leads to faster skill acquisition than longer spacing (one minute to two and a half minutes) between opportunities (Neil & Jones, 2015).
- A faster pace plus more learning opportunities often results in faster acquisition. If your child needs to learn a particular skill quickly (such as learning to say, "Trick or treat," for Halloween), then more opportunities more closely spaced makes sense.
- If you begin to teach a skill in one context and your child is not making progress, consider teaching the skill in another context. You can begin instruction of that skill in both contexts simultaneously or switch entirely to a different context.

We have illustrated how instruction can be provided both more formally and during ongoing activities. When you begin instruction with your little one, you will address a range of different skills in all of these different contexts. That means you may teach your child using more intensive and less intensive instruction, depending on the skill. Realize also that the context in which you address a skill area may change over time. For example, when you first teach motor imitation, you may start with a relatively intense intervention and provide many opportunities, closely spaced, with several sessions each week. However, as your child learns to imitate, you may only need to provide a few opportunities for your child to learn new motor imitation skills, reflecting more naturalistic instruction.

When you need to provide formal instruction (e.g., to work on more difficult skills, when you want to provide many repeated opportunities closely spaced, when your child needs a distraction-free environment, etc.), pick a special place that has relatively few distractions. Otherwise, teach throughout the day in the situations in which you and your child find yourselves—at the park, at the library, out to lunch, when visiting Grandma, while reading before naptime, etc.

Checking for Maintenance

When children continue to use the skills they have learned, it is referred to as *maintenance*. You can determine if your child has maintained skills simply by providing him with an opportunity to perform the skill. This is referred to as a ***probe***. During probes, present the S^D and then wait for your child to independently engage in the behavior, but do not provide any prompts. Usually, probes involve just one or two opportunities rather than a session of many repeated opportunities. Probes can serve several purposes; you may present probe opportunities to check for maintenance, generalization, and to see if your child already knows a skill and you do not need to teach it.

When you present a maintenance probe opportunity, you will know your child has maintained the skill if he responds correctly. If your child does not correctly perform the behavior, this could mean that he no longer has the skill in his repertoire. You can provide another opportunity using the least-to-most prompting strategy described earlier in the chapter. If your child continues to need prompts to perform the behavior, you may have to teach it again. Fortunately, it is likely that he will learn the skill quicker the second time around.

It is important to conduct maintenance probes on a regular basis. As we described in Chapter 2, children with Down syndrome may show inconsistent performance, so regular practice can be important to increase consistency. We suggest conducting maintenance probes once per week. You can even assign a day on which you just run maintenance probes (e.g., every Monday). Decide on a schedule and note it on the Program Planner.

HOW TO HANDLE BEHAVIOR THAT INTERFERES WITH LEARNING

So far in this chapter, we have talked about how to teach new skills (increase behaviors). But there are also behaviors we want to decrease. We refer to such behaviors as *behaviors that interfere with learning*. They may also be referred to as *inappropriate or undesirable behaviors* and sometimes as *problem* or *challenging behaviors*. Consider a girl who is learning to color but throws the crayons and never actually uses them. She will not have an opportunity to learn to color. Consider a boy who is learning to put his shoes on but screams when his mother approaches with the shoes. He never gets a chance to learn to put his shoes on. These types of behaviors interfere with learning and could potentially prevent a child from becoming an independent adult.

HANNAH ~ Behavior That Interferes with Learning. When Hannah's mom was teaching her to clean up, Hannah sometimes refused to do so when asked. Sometimes she would sit on the floor, cross her arms, and refuse to do anything, and other times she would be silly and put things away in all the wrong places—her socks in the car basket, her cars in the drawer for her shirts, etc.

Reinforcement Also Happens with Interfering Behaviors

One of the most challenging concepts for caregivers (including our own spouses and family members) to understand is that, when behaviors—even those we consider problematic or inappropriate—are followed by consequences that the child likes, those behaviors increase. The aspect that is difficult to understand is that what one person prefers may be very different from what another person prefers. For example, the eldest son of one of the authors loved attention as a young child. He would often sing, dance, or tumble on the floor to gain the attention of both of his parents, who readily smiled, clapped, praised, and hugged their son. But occasionally he would head toward an electric outlet with one of his toys, as if he was going to stick it into the socket. Of course, his parents' immediate response was to stop everything, go to him, and say, "No, no, that is dangerous!" In both situations, they stopped what they were doing, looked at him, and interacted with him in a social manner—albeit, one situation resulted in his parents being frightened and alarmed. However, from this little guy's perspective, that did not matter; they were paying attention to him. The effect was that both behaviors, singing/dancing and attempting to put things in electric outlets, increased, because both resulted in reinforcing consequences (i.e., attention).

For most children, and particularly those with Down syndrome, social attention is a powerful positive reinforcer that can be used to develop and increase a variety of important behaviors. Yet, as in our example, providing social attention can also reinforce or increase undesirable or inappropriate behaviors.

HANNAH ~ Positive Reinforcement of Interfering Behaviors. When Hannah refused to clean up, her mom tried to cajole Hannah into cleaning up. She would say things like, "Come on Hannah, let's clean up. Maybe we should sing the clean-up song." This usually got Hannah going again, for a little bit, but then she would sit down again, sometimes even hiding behind the couch, and refuse to clean up. Her mother would then repeat the entire sequence.

What was going on with Hannah? When Hannah refused to clean up, her mom gave her lots of attention to try to cajole her into cleaning up. What do you think is going to happen to Hannah's refusal to clean up in the future? If you think it is probably going to increase, you are right. Because social attention functioned as a reinforcer for Hannah, Hannah's refusal is likely to increase.

As you know, behaviors also increase as a result of negative reinforcement (the removal of a nonpreferred stimulus as a consequence for a behavior). This applies to both desirable and undesirable behaviors—both can be increased as a result of negative reinforcement.

HANNAH ~ Negative Reinforcement of Interfering Behaviors. Hannah's mother was sometimes in a rush to get out of the house, so one day, instead of cajoling her daughter when she got silly cleaning up her toys, she just cleaned up the toys herself, following behind Hannah as she put toys in the wrong places and putting them in the right places. Then the next day, Hannah again put her toys and things in the wrong places when cleaning up, and her mother did the same thing, because they were on their way out of the house to a dentist appointment. Hannah was learning that if she did not clean up her toys correctly, her mother might pay attention to her or clean up the toys for her.

So now, when Hannah refused to clean up her toys or put them in the wrong place, she sometimes got positive reinforcement in the form of social attention and sometimes got out of cleaning up her toys. Remember, this is negative reinforcement, because the demand to clean up was taken away (negative) and Hannah's refusal increased (reinforcement).

Let's look at another example of negatively reinforcing an undesirable behavior. A child was fidgeting, teasing the children on either side of her, and standing up in the middle of circle time. As this was disruptive, the teacher's first reaction was to send the girl back to her desk, away from the group. The teacher then wondered why her student's behavior during circle time did not improve.

Let's break this down a bit. The interfering behaviors were fidgeting, talking to other children, and standing up during circle time. When the child engaged in the interfering behaviors, the teacher sent her away from the group, removing the demands of the group activity. Then, the next day, the girl engaged in the exact same behaviors during the group activity. This is a classic example of negative reinforcement; the group demands were removed (the negative part), and the child still engaged in the same behavior. Removing the girl from the group was actually reinforcing her interfering behaviors because leaving the group activity was a pleasurable consequence.

In this situation, the teacher may have thought she was punishing the child and that sending her away from the group activity was going to decrease the interfering behaviors. Remember, punishment is any consequence that results in a *decrease* in the preceding response. However, the teacher was actually reinforcing the girl's interfering behavior, since her actions *increased* the girl's behaviors. Remember, the negative part of negative reinforcement does not have to do with whether you think what happened after a behavior was good or bad. Instead the negative part means you are taking something away. But if behavior increases, the consequence was reinforcement.

Responding to Your Child's Behavior That Interferes with Learning

Like all children do, your child with Down syndrome will engage in some behaviors you will want to increase and other behaviors that you would like to decrease or even never see again. Handling this sort of behavior that interferes with learning includes (1) responding when that behavior occurs and (2) teaching your child more appropriate behaviors.

Do you remember how to respond when your child makes an incorrect response? Well, interfering behavior is just another incorrect response. So, one of the first things to be sure to do is to *not reinforce* that interfering behavior. The technical term for no longer providing reinforcement following a previously reinforced response is *extinction.*

HANNAH ~ Responding to Behavior That Interferes with Learning. Hannah's mother had been inadvertently reinforcing her daughter's challenging behaviors by providing a lot of attention and letting her daughter out of cleaning up when she refused or put things away in the wrong places. Hannah's mother decided to put her daughter's refusal and silly behavior on extinction. She no longer cajoled Hannah into cleaning up when she refused or put things away incorrectly and she no longer cleaned up for Hannah. Instead, she used prompting procedures she had used when teaching Hannah to clean up and did so while providing minimal social interaction. Once Hannah cleaned up, her mother provided lots of social attention.

For children with Down syndrome, social attention may be such a powerful reinforcer that it is particularly important, as in Hannah's case, to be sure you do not provide any attention for interfering behavior. Interfering behavior can also increase because of other reinforcing consequences. Think of a child screaming in the check-out line at the grocery store whose mother gives him a treat from the check-out display. Next time they go to the grocery store, what do you think will happen? The child will probably scream, and his mother will probably give him a treat. The undesirable behavior increases because the child receives positive reinforcement (a candy bar) when he screams. If the mother stops giving her child a treat when he screams for it, she is using extinction.

One thing to keep in mind when you use extinction is that the behavior may get worse before it gets better! Unfortunately, this tends to happen. In the beginning, you may see an increase in the rate and/or intensity of the behavior. This is referred to as an *extinction burst.* This typically happens because, at first, the child will make an extra effort to obtain the reinforcer that he was accustomed to receiving. Think back to when you were young and knocked on the door of a friend's house or apartment. Knocking on the door had a history of getting access to your friend (reinforcement). If you knocked once and no one answered, what would you do? Would you just walk away, or would you knock several more times and with more force? You probably chose the latter. This is an example of an extinction burst. Because your knocks were previously reinforced by the appearance of your friend, when knocking was not reinforced (i.e., no one answered the door), it often resulted in a burst of the behavior (in this case, knocking rapidly and with more force). But, if continued knocking still did not result in your friend's appearance (the reinforcing consequence), then what? You eventually stopped knocking. Thus, when a behavior no longer results in reinforcement, the behavior eventually decreases.

Here are some tips for implementing extinction:

- Inform everyone in the child's environment (e.g., caregivers, teachers, siblings, etc.) that you are putting a behavior on extinction and that they should initially expect to see an increase in the behavior.
- Make sure everyone in the child's environment does not reinforce the behavior, even though it may become difficult to avoid doing so.
- Everyone needs to be sure not to provide reinforcement for *every* instance of the behavior.
- If the behavior becomes harmful to the child or those around him, provide as little attention as possible (so you do not add a reinforcer) as you ensure the safety of your child and others.
- Provide the child with a more appropriate way to get the reinforcer, as discussed next.

HELPFUL HINT **Be Sure Not to Reinforce during Extinction Bursts**

One potential problem with extinctions bursts is that, in many instances, others in the child's environment will give in and reinforce the escalating interfering behavior during the extinction burst. Unfortunately, when that happens, the child may then learn that the best way to get the desired reinforcer is to engage in the higher rate or intensity of the behavior, an outcome that is the opposite of what was intended.

Think about the child who persistently asked his mother for a treat in the store. While his mother initially ignored him, after he began to cry and yell louder over and over again for the treat, she gave in and got it for him. The child learned that in order to get what he wanted, he needed to yell that he wanted it over and over again. By only reinforcing yelling, his mother ended up differentially reinforcing more intense and higher rates of an interfering behavior. This means that she was only providing her child with reinforcement for more intense and high rates of the behavior, and not low or no rates of the behavior, making the interfering behavior worse.

Teach More Appropriate Behavior

Reinforcement is powerful. We can withdraw it to decease a behavior (as in extinction), and we can provide it to increase more appropriate behavior. That is what we spent the whole beginning of this chapter talking about. We should use both of these strategies all the time—we provide social attention for desirable behaviors, such as doing homework, cleaning up, and playing appropriately with siblings and, at the same time, we do not provide attention for undesirable behaviors, such as not finishing homework, leaving toys on the floor, and ignoring siblings' requests to play. This is differential reinforcement in everyday life. There are several different ways that differential reinforcement can be used to increase more appropriate behavior (and decrease interfering behavior).

When using *differential reinforcement of alternative behaviors (DRA)*, you identify a behavior you will reinforce that is an alternative to the behavior you want to decrease. DRA combines reinforcement for a more appropriate behavior and extinction of the interfering behavior.

Let's revisit the child who screamed in the check-out line at the grocery store. The child's mother decided to teach him to ask for a treat by saying, "Treat, please?" She prompted her son by modeling what to say, and then, once he asked politely, the mother let her child pick a treat for after dinner. Remember, the other thing the mother was doing was no longer giving her child a treat when he screamed in the grocery store (i.e., extinction). (This is also known as *functional communication training*, a common application of DRA in which children are taught more acceptable ways to communicate their desires; discussed in detail in Book 2, Chapter 4.)

Differential reinforcement of incompatible behaviors (DRI) is similar to a DRA procedure in that reinforcement is delivered following a more appropriate behavior. In this case, the behavior that results in reinforcement cannot be done at the same time as the response you would like to decrease. For example, a child twirls small items in her hands repetitively. Her parents decide to provide social attention only when she places her hands in her pockets (a behavior that is incompatible with twirling).

When using *differential reinforcement of the omission of behavior (DRO)* (also referred to as *differential reinforcement of other behavior*), reinforcement is provided when the child does *not* engage in the interfering behavior for a certain period of time or during a prespecified number of tasks.

Remember the child who fidgeted, talked to other children, and stood up during a group lesson? Her teacher used DRO by providing her with a small piece of candy (reinforcement) every minute she was not fidgeting, talking, or standing up.

HANNAH ~ Teach More Appropriate Behavior. Hannah's mother used differential reinforcement of incompatible behaviors—in this case, cleaning up. When

Hannah cleaned up (putting things in the correct places), her mother provided praise (positive reinforcement) (and, at first, access to the iPad). Also, as you may recall, she said, "You did such a great job cleaning up all the cars, I'll put away all the musical instruments so you don't have to," removing the additional cleaning demands (negative reinforcement). Hannah's mother also placed Hannah's refusal to clean up and putting things in the wrong places on extinction. Hannah responded to her mother's first attempts at extinction by trying to leave the room and then escalating to crying and yelling. But, Hannah's mother expected this extinction burst and was prepared to work through some more difficult behavior the first few times she implemented extinction. Fortunately, when Hannah's mother used extinction in combination with reinforcement for incompatible behavior (DRI), Hannah only refused a few more times.

Now that you have a handle on the basic instructional strategies, we can delve into how to make behaviorally based intervention happen for your child.

Chapter 4

MAKING IT HAPPEN

Collaborating Successfully

The families and professionals who have implemented behaviorally based instruction as described in this manual have done so in different ways. How they proceeded depended on several factors, including family and child needs, available resources, and the ways that early intervention, preschool, and kindergarten services were delivered in their communities. Because systems vary widely, there really is not one single "best" way to use this approach.

Despite differences in how communities in the US provide services to children with disabilities, there are also important similarities. First, children with Down syndrome almost always qualify for special education or therapeutic services (physical therapy, speech-language therapy, etc.). And with those services comes an individualized program that delineates goals, services the child will receive, and placement (where services are provided). For infants and toddlers in early intervention (for ages birth through three), this plan is known as an Individualized Family Service Plan (IFSP). For children ages three to twenty-one, the plan is called an Individualized Education Program (IEP).

Second, when a child receives early intervention or special education services, her caregivers need to collaborate with a variety of professionals, including educators and therapists. Parents and professionals meet as a committee at least annually to develop the child's individualized program. The term used to describe these committees varies by region. For example, in some regions they are referred to as IEP teams, and in other regions they are referred to as committees on special education. These groups of individuals make decisions regarding goals, services, and placement and usually communicate with one another throughout the year about the child's progress and other concerns.

As you work your way through this chapter, we will discuss how to gather a group of individuals to implement the programs described in this manual, and we will refer to them as your child's *team*. Now, the individuals who are part of your child's team may or may not be part of the decision-making committee just described. Let us return to Jeremy's and Megan's families, the Gardners and Breens, to see how they each put together a team to work with their child.

Gardner Family	Breen Family
Jeremy Gardner was an only child, and while his dad had a 9 to 5 job, his mother worked from home. The Gardner family chose to have Jeremy receive early intervention services within their home during the first several months. Later Jeremy attended a local community center. The Gardners lived near Jeremy's paternal grandparents, who provided lots of support.	Megan Breen was the youngest of three children; one sister was five and one was seven. Both parents worked outside of the home, so during the early intervention and preschool years, Megan attended day care three days per week at her father's workplace. She spent the other two days each week with her maternal grandmother. Megan also had two college-age aunts who just adored spending time with her.

In this chapter we discuss who might be involved in implementing interventions with a child with Down syndrome and decisions about the services a child receives. In many instances, several different people are involved, so understanding their roles and the professions they represent can be helpful. We will also discuss strategies for collaborating and other resources that may help as you put this approach in place.

Putting Together a Team

The team responsible for implementing your child's instructional program should include parents and/or other family members, as well as a variety of professionals. These professionals may include (1) early interventionists or preschool or kindergarten teachers; (2) physical, occupational, or speech therapists or other professionals with specialized expertise (referred to as *related service providers*); and (3) childcare providers (e.g., daycare provider, babysitter, etc.). The members of the team may work either directly or indirectly with your child with Down syndrome to enhance her development. Now, teams will look different depending upon family values, places the child goes (e.g., childcare), and the way intervention services are provided within your community. Again, this team of individuals may or may not be part of the decision-making committee that determines whether your child is in need of services and which services she may require.

Although this manual is designed so that any team can use it to develop a comprehensive program, it is important for at least one of the team members to be a *behavior analyst* or have extensive training and experience in behavior analysis. The person may be certified by the national certification body (Behavior Analysis Certification Board) and/or be licensed as a behavior analyst (if that license exists in your state). For certification and licensure, a professional must have passed rigorous coursework and a comprehensive exam and have participated in supervised experience implementing behavior analytic interventions. The most important role that a behavior analyst will play is making adjustments when the current teaching strategies do not result in improvements. A behavior analyst can

- evaluate the consequences in place to ensure that they are in fact reinforcing,
- determine which skills to teach and in which order,
- determine whether a more intensive approach to instruction is warranted, and
- ensure that an effective behavior plan is developed in the event behaviors are interfering with learning.

To find a behavior analyst in your area, you can search the online directories of the Behavior Analysis Certification Board and Association for Behavior Analysis International (see Appendix B). You can also try contacting your local colleges and universities. One or more may have a teacher preparation program or psychology department that can provide you with information about finding a behavior analyst. More and more provider agencies and school districts are specifically hiring behavior analysts, so you may just need to ask for that person to be on your team. If not, check with your health insurance company to see whether the services of a behavior analyst are covered, and if so, what sort of out-of-pocket costs may be involved.

Here are some other important points to consider when putting together your child's team:

- Parents and/or other family members are the most important members of the team, although the extent to which each is interested in or able to take an active role in implementing intervention will vary. We recommend considering immediate family members (i.e., parents and siblings), as well as extended family, and even close friends who may be great resources. A twenty-year-old cousin in college may be the perfect person to help with your child's interventions an afternoon or two each week; Grandma may happily work in teaching each time she cares for your child.

- If your child attends a day care center or community preschool where personnel are open to using these procedures, they too can provide intervention during the course of the day. Sometimes children attend a community preschool with a special education teacher (often referred to as *special education itinerant services*) or teacher's assistant who can implement intervention.

- If your child attends an early intervention or preschool program that serves many children with disabilities in the same location (referred to as a *center-based program*), personnel are often accustomed to providing individualized interventions.

- Some providers of early intervention or preschool special education deliver direct services (the professional or therapist works directly with the child for a specified length of time and number of sessions per week or month). If this is the case in your community, any of those service providers can implement intervention. If direct services are not provided in your area, then professionals will provide parent training to help parents implement intervention. In this case, the responsibility will be on family members, making it particularly important to incorporate these interventions into daily routines.

- Think outside the box. There are probably people within the community who may be very motivated to learn how to teach your child. Think about high school students in need of community service hours, a senior citizen who is interested in spending time with children, or a college student who wants experience.

Understanding Perspectives about Intervention for Children with Down Syndrome

The many members of your team will likely have many different perspectives regarding how young children with disabilities (Down syndrome, in this case) should be educated. You see, applied behavior analysis is but one perspective regarding how to provide intervention to children with Down syndrome. For most

Gardner Family	Breen Family
Jeremy's family was creative in putting together a team. During his toddler years, they needed an extra set of hands to implement his instructional programs at home. So his mother asked a community college to post a flyer asking for volunteers interested in gaining (unpaid) experience working with a toddler with Down syndrome. Two students majoring in psychology each agreed to come a morning a week to work with Jeremy.	There were several people on Megan's team. When she was three years old, her mother asked Jacklyn, a neighborhood teenager, to help with Megan's toilet training. She paid her the going hourly rate for a teenage babysitter. Megan's aunts also came to help because they loved to spend time with her. Each came during the afternoons for three weeks, sitting with Megan, waiting for her to use the toilet. This allowed her mother to spend afternoons with her two daughters while giving Megan consistency during toilet training.
During the preschool years, Jeremy continued to receive services at his community center but in an integrated preschool class (one that had children with and without disabilities). There were monthly team meetings at which family, classroom staff, and related service personnel met to review Jeremy's progress on goals.	For preschool, Megan remained at the childcare center where her dad worked. Her parents were persistent in requesting the use of behavior analytic programming. So, her school district made sure the special education teacher on the team had a strong background in applied behavior analysis. This teacher designed instruction embedded within activities that all team members implemented and developed a plan to prevent Megan from engaging in interfering behavior. Speech, occupational, and physical therapies were provided on a consultative basis to the preschool staff.
At the first meeting, the team decided that some of Jeremy's teaching programs would be implemented within discrete trial teaching (many teaching opportunities right in a row), and other instruction would be embedded within routine activities (e.g., at snack, during music, etc.).	

(Continued on next page)

(Continued from previous page)

> Megan continued to spend two days a week with her grandmother, including one day attending a library program with her same-age cousin. Also, Megan's parents continued to set aside thirty minutes each week to work on individual programs. One of Megan's college-age aunts who was studying psychology came by twice a week and also implemented programs. She loved the experience!

parents and other family members, ideas regarding how children should be raised and educated come from our own upbringing, watching other parents, and reading books and articles. For professionals, perspectives regarding how children learn and how they should be educated may also stem from their professional preparation programs (at their colleges or universities), where they are often trained in one theoretical perspective about how children learn.

If you have read Chapter 2, you are aware of our theoretical perspective: applied behavior analysis, which, simply stated, attributes a child's learning to the way she responds to environmental stimuli and the consequences that follow those responses. Here are a few other perspectives:

- A *constructivist* approach attributes children's learning to their ability to problem solve and build their own knowledge based on interactions with their environment.
- A *social learning* approach attributes children's learning to their ability to observe others in their environment.
- A *developmental* approach attributes children's learning to their passage through a series of stages that build upon each other.

Theoretical perspectives are important to consider because they often influence the interventions a professional recommends and provides. For example, the strategies recommended by a professional who follows a constructivist approach may rely on child-directed opportunities (those that are initiated by the child). He or she may encourage children to independently engage with materials so they can actively participate in problem solving and thus *construct* their own knowledge by building on previous experiences. Now, not all professionals adhere to one approach. Some take bits and pieces from more than one perspective, using strategies from each that they find particularly appealing. At the same time, you may meet professionals who do not claim to have any one perspective; however, they may still have strong opinions about how children learn.

Sometimes when professionals work in a group (e.g., at a specialized school or agency), they may all share the same perspective. Even if a therapist works independently, teaching a child in a home or community setting, he or she will likely adhere to a particular perspective. But just because someone takes a specific perspective does *not* mean there is evidence to support the interventions. So, even without any evidence that a strategy is effective, it may still be recommended by professionals who work with a child. And some professionals may be so dedicated to their perspective that they are unwilling to try other strategies.

You may be asking yourself, "What's the big deal? What difference does it make what perspective an interventionist follows?" The fact is, there are very important decisions that are made that are influenced by these different perspectives.

Decisions about How Related Services Should Be Delivered

When a child qualifies for special education services in the United States, she is entitled to developmental, corrective, or other supportive services to help her benefit from special education. (This is thanks to the federal special education law known as the Individuals with Disabilities Education Act, or IDEA.) These services are referred to as *related services*. Speech-language therapy, physical therapy, and occupational therapy are just three of the many related services that a child may have as part of her educational program. There are different ways, referred to as *models*, that these services may be delivered. Choosing a model is an important decision to make as you implement the programs in this manual.

In a *multidisciplinary model*, professionals with expertise in different related services work directly with the child and family but do so independently of each other. Each professional conducts his or her own assessment and then independently develops and provides intervention. This model allows for the child to have direct contact with each of a variety of professionals. However, a lack of coordination between service providers may result in several possibly conflicting interventions being provided to a child and conflicting suggestions being given to a family. For example, an occupational therapist may teach foundational skills to enhance hand strength before teaching writing letters. In contrast, the special educator may immediately start to teach the different strokes that are used to form the letters.

In an *interdisciplinary model*, related service professionals also conduct individual assessments and independently develop and implement intervention plans. But unlike in the multidisciplinary model, the members of the child's team meet regularly to ensure there is a coordinated plan in place. For example, a child's speech-language therapist, special education teacher, and occupational therapist may meet monthly to discuss ways they are working on skills. These efforts to coordinate services are helpful, but on an ongoing basis, developmental areas are likely to be addressed in isolation (e.g., the speech-language therapist works only on communication goals, the physical therapist only on motor goals, etc.). As a result, different and conflicting strategies may continue to be used.

In a *transdisciplinary model*, a team of professionals work together to assess your child's needs and develop and provide interventions. A primary service provider is chosen to work with the family and implement intervention with the child. The professionals on the team practice *role release*. In role release, professionals impart their expertise to the primary service provider, who then carries out the interventions. This prevents fragmented services and allows for streamlined communication with family members and more coherent intervention plans (King, Strachan, Tucker, Duwyn, Desserud, & Shillington, 2009). For example, instead of the speech-language therapist, special education teacher, and occupational therapist each providing intervention for a child, one service provider implements all direct intervention services while being guided with input from the other providers.

Except in complicated situations (e.g., a child has health concerns, swallowing disorders, or very severe motor impairments), we recommend a transdisciplinary approach. It allows the individuals who are with the child the most to understand how to teach goals across developmental areas. Specific goals are not just being addressed when a particular therapist sees the child; all of the goals are addressed throughout the day. When a child enters school, a transdisciplinary approach decreases the amount of time she spends out of the classroom in individual therapy sessions, which may be a problem with a multidisciplinary model. Multidisciplinary models tend to rely on "pull-out" services. For example, in a multidisciplinary approach, a speech-language therapist might remove a child from class to work on speech, and then a physical therapist might take the child out of class to practice walking up and down steps. In contrast, with a transdisciplinary approach, the speech and physical therapists would teach classroom staff and caregivers strategies to teach specific skills within the classroom and at home. Ideally this would be done in person, with the therapist modeling the strategy and observing the other team members' implementation and then providing feedback. This approach allows for speech, stair-climbing, and other important skills to be addressed throughout the day while the child is in the classroom and at home.

Gardner Family	Breen Family
When Jeremy was very young, he received services at home, including speech and physical therapy. His parents also received parent training. When Jeremy was a little older, he began attending the local community center, where he received early intervention services. Families brought their children to the center to receive related services with a combination of parent training and direct services. Twice a week, Jeremy received speech therapy directly from the speech-language therapist, and physical therapy from a physical therapist. Then, once per month, his parents and/or grandparents attended a third session, where they received parent training conducted by each of the therapists and a special educator.	In Megan's community, early intervention services were provided on a consult basis, which means no direct services were provided. Instead, Megan's caregivers received monthly visits from an early interventionist, who provided them with training. During the early intervention years, Megan's parents and other caregivers, including her aunts, grandmother, and daycare personnel, worked through intervention programs like the ones described in Book 2 of this manual. Each worked with Megan for twenty minutes a day, three to four days per week, and documented her performance. They each shared video recordings of themselves working with Megan so they could be sure they were all implementing intervention consistently. They also made sure all the toys and materials were in Megan's bag that went with her from place to place.

Decisions about Direct or Consultant Services for Your Child

When providing *direct services*, the professional works directly with the child and does so either one-on-one (a 1:1 ratio) or in a group (e.g., 3:1 child-to-therapist ratio). When providing *consultant services*, each therapist meets with the child's other team members to teach them what they should be doing to enhance the child's development of a specific set of skills (e.g., speech, motor, etc.). Often, the decision about direct versus consultant services is made based on the model used for providing related services in your area. In schools in which a transdisciplinary model is used, consultant services are quite common. In schools in which a multidisciplinary model is used, we rarely see consultant services. However, you can certainly request consultant services or a combination of both.

Decisions about When a Child Is "Ready" to Learn a Particular Skill

When you think about development, you probably think about children acquiring skills in a certain order, an order that is common for children. For the most part, this is true, as children who are typically developing tend to learn skills at similar ages and in a similar order. For example, children are likely to say simple sounds before multiword phrases and to stand before they run.

Some professionals firmly believe that development happens in a particular order, and for them, that means children *must* learn certain prerequisite skills before they can be taught others. For example, some professionals may teach children to identify individual letters of the alphabet before teaching any other reading skills (e.g., before teaching a child to identify sight words or to identify the sound a particular letter makes). However, if we wait for children to show prerequisite skills to participate in everyday childhood activities such as using riding toys, drawing, and coloring, the child may be well beyond childhood years before she learns those skills (if ever).

As an alternative to this prerequisite approach, we take an *acquisitional* approach to intervention that calls for instruction to take place while the child is engaged in the activity. To continue with the example of sight word reading, we often teach sight words before children have learned all their letters, because reading sight words is often an area of relative strength for children with Down syndrome (likely due to strengths in visual processing). Teaching sight words early helps the child to understand the reading process, and those words can then be incredibly effective prompts (as you learned in Chapter 3) to increase a variety of other skills, most notably expressive language. Of course, all the while we are teaching sight word reading, we continue to teach individual letters and their corresponding sounds.

Sometimes professionals will want to focus on underlying deficits that might explain why a child has difficulty in a given skill area. For example, if a child cannot cut with scissors, some professionals may look for an underlying problem such as low muscle tone, trouble keeping her hands in the middle of her body, or poor eye-hand coordination. This approach has the potential to shift the focus of intervention from cutting (the goal) to hand strength (a presumed cause for poor cutting). So, hours of intervention may be spent trying to improve low muscle tone by doing exercises or engaging in activities that are meant to improve muscle tone, but not within a functional skill such as actually cutting with scissors. In the end, your child may not learn the functional skill at all (i.e., cutting with scissors).

Keep in mind, some aspects of Down syndrome may be present for your child's entire life. Low muscle tone may be one. Working on muscle tone is important, because it affects so many other areas, but not if it means doing so without ever teaching your child the skills she needs to use every day, such as cutting, brushing teeth, writing, etc. As an alternative, we look at underlying characteristics such as low muscle tone for information about how we should tailor intervention to improve functional skills. For example, to teach cutting with scissors, we may begin with scissors that are easier to squeeze and provide physical prompts versus modeling prompts to compensate for the low muscle tone. We design intervention that recognizes the underlying factors that may affect skill acquisition, but we teach those skills while simultaneously addressing the underlying factor—which is another characteristic of an acquisitional approach.

Decisions about What Can Be Used as a Reinforcer

Some perspectives about how children learn suggest that children should be *intrinsically* motivated to engage in certain behaviors—that learning should be its own reward and no external rewards should be used (e.g., a treat or play time with a toy). In general, we use social interaction as a consequence to enhance responding in children with Down syndrome. But we also use tangible items (including food), play activities (e.g., time on a swing), or just some good old free time as reinforcers. Some caregivers are concerned about the use of food in particular as a reinforcer. However, food has the potential to be a very powerful reinforcer, and a child may learn difficult responses more quickly if food is used as a consequence. Also, if used occasionally as reinforcement for difficult responses, food will likely function as a novel stimulus, which can also increase its value as a reinforcer. When adding external reinforcers such as a piece of a favorite food or an opportunity to play a game or read a book, the goal is to fade them so that eventually, the natural consequences maintain the child's behavior.

Decisions about Self-Stimulatory or Repetitive Behavior

We first discussed self-stimulatory or repetitive behavior in Chapter 2 of this book. A self-stimulatory behavior is one a child engages in because it results in automatic reinforcement (i.e., as soon as the behavior occurs, it is reinforcing to the child, independent of any other person). All young children engage in some self-stimulatory or repetitive behavior, but these behaviors can be particularly problematic if they persist in young children with Down syndrome. One perspective on self-stimulatory behavior is to allow the child to engage in that behavior because doing so stimulates development. However, we believe that there are more downsides than upsides to behaviors of this nature. Consider a two-year-old who waves her hands in front of her eyes. If she does this frequently, it will likely prevent her from engaging in at least some learning opportunities. Also, as she matures, her behavior is likely to be stigmatizing, as it is something her peers are unlikely to do and may draw undue attention.

In Book 2, Chapters 2–5, we describe strategies for reducing self-stimulatory behavior. The basic approach is to ensure the child is engaging in age-appropriate behaviors (with some leeway in terms of the specific age) by teaching other behaviors, especially more appropriate ways that the child can obtain the same stimulation.

Getting Everyone on Board: Collaboration among Your Child's Team Members

When there are differences among team members, it may take a bit of effort to get everyone to work together, but it will be well worth it. Here are some ways to develop collaborative relationships with team members from diverse perspectives:

- **Build rapport.** It is much easier to work through differences with someone with whom you have a cordial relationship. Spend some time chatting with team members about things other than philosophies, instructional strategies, and services. You may find you have several things in common (e.g., where you went to high school, interest in local events). Once you have established rapport, talking through interventions and services may be much easier and more pleasant.

- **Be respectful.** Just like you (whether a parent or professional), team members work hard to serve the children and families with whom they work. Professionals have dedicated their careers to children with disabilities and invested many resources in honing their skills. So, even if you do not agree with their perspective, it is important not to dismiss it in a manner that makes them feel as if you do not respect them or their work. You will have to go back and do a lot of rapport building if this happens.

- **Recognize and take advantage of strengths.** The knowledge and expertise from different perspectives is crucial in designing the interventions described in this manual—we just might use different intervention strategies and build skills in different ways. For example, in Book 2, Chapters 2–5, we suggested consulting with a speech-language pathologist or occupational or physical therapist. We did this because those professionals have extensive training in the intricacies of communication and motor skill development that can be helpful in designing interventions.

Focus your interactions on the expertise that other professionals can bring to developing your child's interventions. And, make sure you let them know their input is valued (a little reinforcement)! This will help you continue to build a positive relationship with other members of the team.

■ **Share research and resources.** Chapter 2 in this book provides a concise overview of the literature that supports this approach. After reading that chapter, you will be in a position to share that information with other team members. Appendix B provides additional resources about applied behavior analysis you can also share.

■ **Respond positively to criticism.** It may be that a team member has strong (and possibly negative) opinions about the approach described in this manual. It is important for you to know what to say if others quickly dismiss your suggestions to try this approach. Keep in mind, professionals care deeply about the children they serve, but they may not be aware of the potential benefits or they may be misinformed. Here are a few comments that we often hear, along with some information that might help you respond.

"ABA is only for children with autism." In the first two chapters of this book, we discussed the advantages of using applied behavior analysis with children with autism and provided an overview of its effectiveness with children and adults with Down syndrome. Thus, its application in meeting the needs of children with Down syndrome is very likely to yield positive outcomes.

"Children don't need to be treated that way!" In Chapter 2, we described the scientific foundation of applied behavior analysis and the focus on operant behavior (i.e., what a child learns is based on the consequences of his or her behavior). Our procedures therefore entail providing pleasurable consequences to children to increase the behaviors we want them to learn.

Sometimes people who question behavior analytic intervention strategies feel the approach is too similar to how animals are trained and not appropriate for children. Much of the early work in operant learning *was* done with animals, and ongoing experimental work continues with animals. This work provides an extensive body of research to support the principles on which the interventions we describe are based. And we have lots of research that applies these principles to help us understand how children learn.

- **"Try it."** Sometimes we suggest to team members who have different perspectives that we just "try" an intervention while monitoring the child's progress. Then, the team can use the progress-monitoring information to decide whether to continue the intervention or to try something different. This is why the progress tracking procedures outlined in this manual are so important.

- **Respond to suggestions to implement other approaches.** You will likely hear about many different interventions, and others will likely suggest that you try those interventions. Many alternative treatments exist and are often promoted, even those without evidence demonstrating their effectiveness. (Refer to Chapter 2 for more discussion and some of the references for reviews of various interventions.) It is best to be prepared to respond to suggestions about using alternative interventions without empirical support and be careful not to be disrespectful. To get your point across, consider some of the following responses:
  - ➤ "Thank you for the information, but right now, we are going to try this strategy."
  - ➤ "We appreciate your concern. We will certainly give thought to that suggestion."
  - ➤ "Your concern is very much appreciated, and we may consider that in the future."

- **Agree to disagree.** At some point, when working with our colleagues who have different perspectives, we often say, "Let's agree to disagree." You will not be able to get everyone to adopt a behavior analytic approach. But that does not mean you cannot work with those professionals or that they do not bring valuable knowledge to the table. So, agreeing to disagree is a nice way to move on and not waste time trying to change others' views.

Other Resources That May Help You Implement This Approach

As you explore this approach and begin to implement intervention, there are many resources that you may find useful. There are national organizations dedicated to serving individuals with Down syndrome and their families, many of which have local chapters whose members may assist you within your own community. Many communities have local parent groups that early intervention providers may

Gardner Family	Breen Family
The center where Jeremy received early intervention services had not considered behavior analytic programming for young children with disabilities. As a result, his parents and grandparents met with his therapists to share information about this approach. At first, the therapists expressed several concerns: they did not feel comfortable presenting closely spaced teaching opportunities and felt that focusing on specific skills would prevent Jeremy from generalizing them (i.e., using them in other situations).	During the early intervention years, Megan's parents had a wonderful team of professionals who worked collaboratively to implement the type of programs that have now been published in this manual. However, Megan's grandmother often voiced concerns about how reinforcers were being used with Megan. She did not feel comfortable waiting until Megan performed certain behaviors before she let her have her favorite toys or before she sang Megan her favorite songs. She wanted to be a doting grandmother and shower her with lots of attention and her favorite things.
Jeremy's family had a plan. They requested that each therapist (in addition to themselves) choose one skill area and use ABA procedures to teach that one skill for a full month, documenting Jeremy's progress. Then, when they met the next month, they would review Jeremy's progress to determine whether he was learning and generalizing the skills and whether the therapists still had concerns.	Then Megan's grandmother began to notice differences in Megan's development compared to her other grandchildren. At that point she started to see the value in changing the way she interacted with Megan.
Jeremy's parents and grandparents chose to address the skill of object exploration (i.e., manipulating objects) each time they changed Jeremy's diaper and were sure to bring the toys	Megan's grandmother began to wait to provide Megan with all of those wonderful reinforcing interactions until Megan made even slight approximations of the behaviors she was learning. Once her grandmother consistently did this, she immediately started to see changes, although she

(Continued on next page)

(Continued from previous page)

when they went on outings. Jeremy's speech-language pathologist addressed requesting during her individual speech sessions, and Jeremy's physical therapist addressed cruising skills during her individual physical therapy sessions.

At the next monthly meeting, Jeremy had progressed with all three programs. Each therapist conducted probes to see if the skills generalized to other situations. They did! Jeremy's team then decided to continue using a behavior analytic approach as described in this manual for his early intervention years.

did occasionally shower Megan with attention and her favorite things anyway.

know about. Some school districts have special education parent-teacher associations (SEPTAs). You can check a school district's website to see if they have one. There are also national parent initiatives such as Parent to Parent that connect families of children with disabilities.

Resources directly related to applied behavior analysis will be valuable as you proceed with the interventions in this manual and pursue having a behavior analyst on your team. The use of behavior analytic intervention is more commonplace with children with autism spectrum disorder. Contacting parent or professional groups that focus on autism or other disabilities may help you find professionals who are familiar with applied behavior analysis and training opportunities. They can also provide useful advice on navigating the service delivery system within your community.

What If You Do Not Think the Services Are Right for Your Child?

A major reason it is important to build rapport with the members of your child's team is so that disagreements can be handled without challenges. However, some-

Gardner Family	Breen Family
When planning for Jeremy's transition to kindergarten, his parents and grandparents requested the assistance of a behavior analyst. They had spoken with families of children with autism and asked questions about the services their children received. They learned that the district had a behavior analyst who provided consultative services to children who had a diagnosis of autism.	Megan's parents had long been members of the parent-teacher association (PTA) in their district. Each year, volunteers were asked to serve on the district's hiring committee, which was made up of professionals, PTA members, and representatives from the community. As Megan entered kindergarten her parents jumped at the chance to serve on the hiring committee. They knew it was a perfect opportunity to share with the other members of the committee the value of hiring professionals who had strong backgrounds in applied behavior analysis. After Megan's parents presented information on the effectiveness of the approach with students with Down syndrome and other disabilities, the committee agreed this would be a requirement for all new educators working with students with disabilities in the district.
Initially Jeremy's family was told, "The behavior analyst only works with children with autism." As they had done when he was younger, Jeremy's parents shared with the team some of the same information contained in Chapter 2 of this book and the *NYSDOH Clinical Practice Guideline for Down syndrome*. The team agreed that Jeremy's program would benefit from the input of a behavior analyst.	
The behavior analyst joined Jeremy's team and suggested that he receive two thirty-minute sessions of discrete trial teaching conducted by the classroom teaching assistant each school day. His parents also provided at least four more thirty-minute sessions each week in their home. This was in addition to the instructional staff and related service personnel embedding instruction within all classroom activities each day.	

times team members cannot come to an agreement about services for a particular child. As family members, if you are not able to convince service providers to teach your child using behaviorally based programming, consider implementing the programs in your home and/or community and document your child's progress. If you take this approach, we recommend you implement just one of the programs in Book 2, carefully document the child's performance, and share the results with other team members and administrators. We highly recommend video recording your child before and after teaching specific skills using this approach. As you know, a picture (or in this case, a video) is worth a thousand words. Sharing the documentation of your child's progress may convince others to reconsider its use.

If you are not able to convince your team or the committee who makes decisions about goals, services, and placement to try this approach, it is important to know that educational laws in the United States clearly articulate that families have a role in the education of their children, those with and without disabilities. Professionals should realize the importance of family members being made aware of their rights. When families know their rights, it can make all of the difference in ensuring a child receives an appropriate education. Thus, it is *very* important for both families and professionals to be informed regarding federal laws, state regulations, and local guidelines, because schools may not always follow the letter of the law. Within those communities, it is important to become familiar with these documents and/or to work closely with groups who are familiar with them. This may include local parent groups, advocacy organizations, and legal aid organizations (which offer services for free or on a sliding scale based on income).

Getting to Know the Law

Federal Legislation

When providing special education services, each state must follow the federal law—the Individuals with Disabilities Education Act. Part C of IDEA is the section of the law that directly relates to infants and toddlers with disabilities. It is a federal grant program that assists states in operating their statewide early intervention programs for children birth through two years of age and their families. Each state must choose a lead agency to administer the program. The agency varies by state; for example, in some states, the education department is the lead agency, and in other states it is the department of health.

Depending on the governmental agency responsible for overseeing early intervention services, the entities responsible for delivering those services may vary. For example, if the department of education is the responsible entity, local school districts provide early intervention services. If another entity provides early intervention, the services may be provided by agencies not directly affiliated with your local school district. This means there will be some type of transition process between the two systems when your child enters preschool or kindergarten. It is important to find this out when a child is young so that both family members and professionals can prepare for that transition. Administrators of the agency or district that provides services should know who provides early intervention services (Part C of IDEA) in your state. Also, the governor of each state must appoint an interagency council that includes professionals and parents. Some states have local interagency councils. Becoming familiar with the members of the interagency council and attending their meetings can also be helpful.

Part B of IDEA is the section of the law that directly relates to students with disabilities ages three through twenty-one. Preschool special education services (for children ages three to five) are overseen by each state's department of education. However, depending on where you live, preschool services may be provided through your local education agency (i.e., the school district) or through an outside agency (approved by your state education department). If you are in a community that depends on outside providers, that is one more transition that your child and family will need to make before entering kindergarten. Be sure to inquire with other team members and your school district so that relationships can be built early.

Once a child is kindergarten age, the local school district is responsible for providing educational and related services. We recommend checking the school district's website to learn about administrators, school board members, and other important individuals within the district. You are about to enter a long-term relationship with these individuals, and the sooner you establish a rapport with them, the better!

State Legislation and Guidelines

Each state is responsible for developing a set of special education guidelines that correspond to federal legislation (IDEA). States can provide more services than those outlined by the federal law, but they cannot provide fewer. Thus, if a state feels that there are certain provisions that are important for students with disabilities within their state, they can certainly enter them into their guidelines. However, states cannot fail to provide any services that are included in IDEA. The agency responsible for providing services to children birth to age three develops guidelines for this age group. The department of education in each state develops the guidelines for children three to twenty-one years of age.

Quality Assurance Offices

In many states, a quality assurance department oversees the delivery of early intervention and special education services. This department's role is to ensure that agencies or schools providing special education services are in compliance with their state's special education guidelines. Check your state's early intervention program and education department websites for contact information for your quality assurance office. These offices are intended to serve families, so both family members and professionals should feel free to contact this state office in the event questions or concerns arise.

School District Policies

Just as state guidelines must be in compliance with federal law, school district policies must follow their state's guidelines. However, it has been our experience that school districts tend not to develop written policies. This can sometimes be problematic, as it can be difficult for families to be aware of what their individual school district offers—unless district personnel are forthcoming or families within a district have a strong network and share what they have learned about district policies and programs with one another.

Due Process

If a family is not in agreement with a decision made by the committee who creates the individualized plan consisting of goals, services, and placement, they have the right to *due process.* A particular challenge in some communities is having a child with a disability such as Down syndrome educated with typically developing peers. The extent to which a child with a disability has access to typical peers is referred to as the Least Restrictive Environment (LRE). You see, in some communities, children with Down syndrome are automatically placed in special schools or special classes that have only children with intellectual disabilities enrolled. If you feel the programs or services being recommended for your child are not appropriate or are not being implemented in the LRE, you have the right to due process.

Ideally, differences can be resolved through collaboration and appeals to representatives at the district or state level. Some school districts are willing to go to *mediation* (which means an impartial person helps the district and the team come to an agreement), but others may not have this process in place. In the absence of a mediation process, families can make a formal appeal to an impartial officer to review the situation and make a decision. For students with IEPs, the impartial hearing officer is a representative of your state's department of education, but for early intervention, he or she represents the agency that provides early intervention services in your state. The hearing officer's review and decision is made at what is called an *impartial hearing.*

Due process can be quite draining, in terms of energy, emotions, and financial costs, as districts will have an attorney present. Although it is not mandatory that families have legal representation, it is recommended. This is why we strongly suggest reaching out to decision makers early in the process—building a rapport with key people can go a very long way! But, if you find you are in a position in which the issues cannot be resolved, you can contact local advocacy organizations for recommendations for legal counsel as well as educational advocates.

Gardner Family	Breen Family
At the annual meeting, when it was time for decisions to be made regarding the types of services and supports Jeremy should receive in kindergarten, the committee (including Jeremy's parents and grandparents) agreed that Jeremy would attend his local elementary school in a general education classroom. His special education services included a shared teaching assistant in the classroom (who was in the class to support three children who received special education services, including Jeremy) as well as resource room instruction three times per week.	When it was time for Megan to transition from preschool services to kindergarten, the committee decided the best placement was in an integrated class that was taught by both a special educator and a general educator and included students with and without disabilities.
Within the classroom setting, there were several instructional periods (45-minute blocks) in which centers were set up along the perimeter of the classroom and children worked in small groups led by either the teacher, the teaching assistant assigned to the class, or the shared teaching assistant. While in these centers, the teacher or assistant used instruction embedded within an activity. When Jeremy went to the resource room,	At this decision-making meeting, the Breen family requested that Megan's program include some instructional time dedicated to discrete trial teaching. They were promptly informed that, if their child needed that type of instruction, her placement would need to be in a self-contained class (i.e., a class containing only children with disabilities).
	This greatly concerned Megan's parents, because discrete trial teaching is an effective instructional strategy that has research to support its use and they did not understand how its use would warrant a change to a more restrictive placement. Thus, at the decision-making meeting (referred to as the IEP team meeting

(Continued on next page)

(Continued from previous page)

his shared teaching assistant accompanied him. Here he received discrete trial teaching.

Jeremy's related services included occupational therapy, physical therapy, and speech therapy and were provided on a consult basis using a transdisciplinary approach.

in their community), the Breen family informed the members that they were not in agreement and requested to pursue their right to due process.

The Breen family gathered electronic copies of several studies published in peer-reviewed journals and e-mailed them to the other members of their team. Fortunately for the Breens, they did not have to go to due process. After looking at the research, the IEP team members agreed that discrete trial teaching was an evidence-based strategy that could be provided to Megan if she was placed in an integrated class. A second meeting was held to discuss exactly how to incorporate discrete trial teaching into the classroom.

Paving the Way for Other Children

We realize that we have given you a great deal of new information to absorb. Referring back to these chapters will help you as you work your way through Book 2 of this manual. We hope you will keep in mind that, when you use this approach to intervention with your child, you have the potential to do more than just change the outcomes for your son or daughter. You have the potential to lay the groundwork for future children to receive this type of intervention in your community. Simply by sharing information with families and professionals, you can help pave the way for others to more easily access evidence-based interventions for their children with Down syndrome.

Gardner Family	Breen Family
Wow! The Gardner family had a great year! All of Jeremy's therapists loved him, and he made so much progress. The Gardners were convinced it was because everyone was fully aware of the important things to teach Jeremy and, most importantly, how to teach them. What a wonderful team!	Overall, Megan's family was pleased with the way kindergarten year went for Megan. She learned many skills and made several friends. She was often invited to classmates' homes for play dates, and two of the girls in her class were attending the same day camp as Megan the upcoming summer. What a relief this was for Megan's parents, as they knew Megan would be thrilled to see her friends at the camp.
Jeremy accomplished so much: he was communicating more, learned his colors and shapes, and was working hard on his motor skills so that he could better navigate the school building and be more successful in physical education class. His individualized instruction skills were taught in small component parts using discrete trial teaching—this was the key to Jeremy's success.	Over the course of the school year, Megan's mother had established a very nice rapport with Megan's teacher. They often corresponded in Megan's communication book and occasionally touched base over the phone. Also, Megan's mom, dad, or grandmother participated in all of the field trips, class parties, and parent-teacher association (PTA) events. All three were on a first-name basis with many members of the school community (the PTA president, security guards, custodians, other involved parents, etc.).
One of the most rewarding moments came when Jeremy participated in the kindergarten school play and had a speaking part! It was an excellent way for the whole school community to see how the work of a small group of professionals and a room full of five- and six-year-olds could come together to support a child with a disability!	At the annual IEP meeting, Megan's team reviewed her progress; they agreed that she had acquired many skills this school year and had met

(Continued on next page)

(Continued from previous page)

all of her IEP goals. But, surprisingly, a few of the team members once again recommended a self-contained placement. And Megan's teacher was unusually quiet when placement was being discussed.

Once again, Megan's parents made it clear that they did not agree with the placement recommendation. They expressed their belief that the gains Megan had made were substantial enough that the placement should not be changed. Admittedly, they were uncomfortable going against the team's recommendation. But they were glad they did, as at the very end of the meeting, the team members agreed to keep the same placement and supports in place for first grade. Although some team members did not seem happy with this decision, both Megan's parents and her classroom teacher left the meeting smiling!

Chapter 5

SUCCESS STORIES

In this chapter we share the stories of three families who have used behavior analytic intervention to meet the needs of their young children with Down syndrome. The first two are families we are fortunate to have gotten to know and work with over the years. The last is Owen, the first child with whom we implemented this intervention.

Emme Jax's Story

by Emme's Mom (Wanda Jax)

I'm not sure why, but I think I always knew I was going to have Emme. All of the experiences in my life have led me to be a better mom to my children, Emme and Will; a better wife to the most amazing husband, Dennis; a better daughter to my mother, Leia; a better friend; a better employee... and to have a better appreciation of the knowledge needed for advocacy for children with disabilities.

The whirlwind started in 2010, when we learned that Emme might have Down syndrome and were told that she would require surgery right after birth to repair her small bowel. We immediately uprooted our growing family from our newly purchased home. We moved two hours away into an RV—with our then two-year-old son, Will—to ensure that Emme would be born at the best hospital around. We weren't going to take any chances.

We expected the medical staff at the hospital to have an understanding of her needs and to be able to meet them. This expectation would later transfer over to our family and friends and the educational system who would learn to serve her.

Once we got back home from our long hospital stay, in-home Early Start services began. Weekly, Emme had separate interventionists come into our home to work with her. Teachers, speech-language therapists, speech therapists with feeding expertise, occupational therapists, physical therapists—the list goes on. We watched the interventions take place and learned to participate so that we could continue the intervention when the professionals were gone.

During these sessions, Emme's noncompliance with tasks that were difficult for her became very apparent to us. We knew this kid had the ability to learn skills— and to learn them fast—we just couldn't understand why she wasn't doing it.

When Emme began refusing to eat solid foods, we got support from her behaviorist, who developed a behavior plan in collaboration with us and the feeding therapist. Emme immediately began to show significant progress. Emme was eating! No G-tube for this family. This newfound relief got me thinking…might behavioral strategies be effective in *all* areas of Emme's development?

Based on my professional experience, I was already familiar with applied behavior analysis (ABA) for children with autism. I actually live and work in an area that has been very influential in the use of ABA strategies for children with autism. With the dedication of our community—and one mother in particular, Debra, and an amazing coworker, Jirii—I was inspired to support children with disabilities in reaching their potential. So, I started researching ABA services for children with Down syndrome.

After months of contemplating and researching, in December of 2012, we finally asked Emme's Early Start service coordinator for an ABA assessment. Emme was twenty-eight months old.

The ABA assessment contained numerous recommendations, including that Emme would benefit from intervention that was based on the principles of ABA, with an emphasis on multiple learning opportunities (i.e., discrete trial teaching), including errorless learning, reinforcement strategies, backward chaining, prompt fading, and varied instruction, to name a few. The recommended goals addressed deficits in attending, imitation, receptive and expressive language, communication, cognition, school readiness, play and socialization, and self-help skills. We were curious to see if Emme would respond to the ABA teaching strategies in all of these areas of her development.

Needless to say, Emme responded. And she responded well!

From January to May of 2013, with the help of ABA intervention, Emme made impressive gains in her expressive and receptive communication abilities, as well as problem-solving skills, based on the Rating Scale for the Carolina Curriculum for Infants and Toddlers with Special Needs. For example, her expressive communication went from 12 months to 26 months, receptive communication from 16 months to 21 months, and problem solving/reasoning went from 16 months to 26 months. Her overall ratings in communication went from 14 months to 22 months, and her overall cognitive rating went from 21 months to 27 months. And all this happened within four short months.

So what did all of this really mean for us? It meant that ABA intervention was extremely effective for Emme in addressing the behavioral characteristics of Down syndrome. It meant that Emme was using verbal communication. Within two weeks of starting ABA, Emme completely stopped using the nonverbal baby signs that our family had taught her. She was spontaneously saying, "Milk," "More," "Bubbles," "Help," and so on. The ABA program taught her that words were important and she could use them to navigate her world!

I began to see Emme's world change. I watched her go up to kids out in the community and say "Hi," and to my delight, they said "Hi" back. In response to this, she would giggle or say "Ball"—and the kids would start to play ball with her. For the first time as a mother to this amazing little girl, I was able to hear her say the words "I love you."

Emme began to learn more from her surroundings by *exploring* them, rather than waiting for the world to come to her. Emme was willing to work harder for tasks that, only weeks and months before, she would have given up on. The ABA strategies were working in all aspects of her learning, and they were working for us. We worked hard to understand how to implement the strategies and made sure that our family and friends also understood. We applied the strategies to everything: bathing, washing hands, cleaning up after a meal, brushing her own hair, folding clothes, answering how old she was when someone asked her, staying with us while out in the community, playing Sofia the First matching game, and—most recently—swimming. We even used the strategies on our son and the neighborhood kids. ABA worked with everyone!

The ABA strategies supported Emme in every niche of her life. She continued to make notable gains in all areas of her development. The three areas where ABA had the most impact for Emme were feeding skills/eating, receptive and expressive communication, and compliant behavior. But, all of the skills and abilities that Emme developed with ABA programming have prepared her for inclusive educational programming.

Emme can now tell the other students, "Play bubbles, guys," "Play tea party," or "No, I don't want to"—her favorite sentence. Emme can sit during circle time, eat lunch with her peers, and attend to academic and table-time tasks. When asked to do a task, Emme has learned that she has to try to complete it—even if it's hard—because her *entire* team (family and friends included) has had that expectation of her and has followed through consistently.

And now, here we are: kindergarten in the fall. Emme is almost six years old. This is what we have been preparing for, for the last three and a half years. Emme will be attending the same school as her big brother. We still almost can't believe it. Emme attending school with her big brother is all we have ever wanted for her—and for him! And only one school calendar to organize? Hallelujah! As parents we had spent many hours preparing for Emme's educational meetings, making sure that her entire team knew what we knew—that Emme would (and *could*) benefit from inclusive education.

Luckily, we have found an amazing educational team that is willing to be creative and to collaborate with us to ensure that we are all meeting Emme's needs. The school team *wants* Emme at their school. They understand that Emme has needs and that as a team we will need to ensure the appropriate supports, including ABA, are in place for her to make progress. Without a collaborative team supporting Emme, we would not have seen this growth in her. What a lucky little girl she is!

Fostering collaboration is not always easy, but it is *key*. We cannot wait to see where Emme will go from here. And, alongside our community, we will be growing and changing with her.

For now, we'll continue to prepare Emme for this transition into her new school. Using ABA strategies (of course), we'll be teaching Emme the song that all of her new classmates will be singing at her new school—hand gestures and all. This way, when all the other kids are doing it, she can join in too. So far, she's mastering it with a smile.

Sarah's Story

by Sarah's Mom (Randy Keady)

Sarah was born in the summer of 2001. She is the youngest of three siblings; her brother, Thomas, had just turned five, and her sister, Kate, was almost three. We wanted three children, so having Sarah felt like completing the picture we had envisioned for our family. Shortly after she was born, the hospital pediatrician asked us questions about our families' histories and informed us that they suspected she had Down syndrome. I felt shock, grief, and guilt. Shock and grief because this was not the vision I had pictured for my family. Guilt because I was not feeling the joy and thrill of motherhood that I felt when I had Thomas and Kate. Rather than delight in the bundle of joy that graced our family, I worried about what her life would be like and how it would change the dynamic of our family. Later that day, we were also told that Sarah had a blood disorder that could be more life threatening if it turned out that she did not have Down syndrome.

The feelings of grief and guilt were quickly replaced by protectiveness and a call to action to figure out how we were going to care for Sarah. During those early days, Sarah's father focused on learning more about Sarah's medical concerns while I focused on learning about trisomy 21 as a syndrome and how it would affect Sarah's development. I was full of questions for the geneticist, who reminded me that first and foremost Sarah was a newborn like her siblings and advised me to care for her as such. This piece of advice set the precedent for treating Sarah like her brother and sister and understanding how to adjust to her having Down syndrome. For example, breastfeeding my children was a priority. Given that babies with Down syndrome have low muscle tone, I had to learn strategies that enabled and strengthened Sarah's ability to nurse. This became my goal as Sarah's mother; my commitment was to nurture her as I did her siblings while learning how having trisomy 21 would necessitate adjustments in that nurturing.

Having children encourages parents to hope and dream about the future. Although some of my hopes and dreams for Sarah are different from those I have for her siblings, the essentials are the same. I want my children to be the best they can be. To do so, they have to learn the value of hard work by doing it, act with integrity, and treat others with respect, kindness, and compassion. I believe that practicing these values will result in a life rich with happiness, a sense of accomplishment, and a feeling of belonging in our community. The question became whether I could help Sarah accomplish these goals in the same way I could for her siblings.

I was born in Taiwan and moved to the United States in 1970. In the mid-1970s, my family moved from a large metropolitan area to a suburb that had few Asian families. My memories of adolescence are unhappy ones because I was made to feel different as a result of being Chinese. I've spent some time over the years thinking about my feelings of grief when I first learned Sarah had Down syndrome. I've come to realize that my grief was not because she had an extra chromosome but rather because I understood the alienating experiences she would most likely have as a result of having Down syndrome. I recalled how I felt as a teenager being made to feel different by peers and adults because of my ethnicity. Upon reflection, I understood how my peers with disabilities must have felt being educated in separate locations and not included in their communities.

As a high school social studies teacher, I tried to envision what school would look like for Sarah. Like most schools where I lived, the school I taught in during the 1990s did not have any students with Down syndrome, and the small number of students with more involved needs (like intellectual disability) were educated in self-contained classes with very limited interactions with typical peers. This visual gave me great anxiety, because I did not want my daughter to grow up feeling different, as I had. I needed to figure out how she was going to be included in her community so she would not grow up feeling more different than like her peers.

Unfortunately, that systemic segregation started in preschool where we live. You see, my older children attended a community preschool, and that was what I wanted for our Sarah. I would never have dreamed of sending my typically developing toddler or preschooler to an out-of-community school transported by a school bus rather than me. Why would I do that with my child with a developmental disability?

When Sarah was two months old, I researched all the special preschools where we lived and set out to visit the ones that I thought might have the best program for her. I have vivid memories of factors that I was considering at that time. How would I juggle my responsibilities to my other children and still drive Sarah to a school that would meet *her* needs? A family member attempted to put my concerns about the school bus to rest by commenting that since Sarah would ride special buses all her life, she might as well learn early and ride one as a toddler. I also recall inquiring at the nursery at the gym I attended whether they could care for Sarah while I was exercising. I was actually asked whether Sarah was a "biter" or a "hugger." A school administrator, out of concern, advised me that the most important skill I could teach Sarah was to sign for help. While I thanked him for his advice, I also questioned in my mind whether this was the most I could expect from my nearly six-month-old daughter. These mental pictures of what I could expect for my daughter made me sad.

The summer that Sarah turned one year old, we attended some Mommy and Me programs at a few special preschools. My goals were to make an informed decision and adjust to the reality that Sarah's nursery/preschool experience was going to look very different from her siblings' experience and that her educational journey would also look different from her peers'. But then I attended a conference sponsored by a local organization founded by families of children with Down syndrome in conjunction with a local university. This conference on best practices in the education of children with Down syndrome was a turning point in my understanding of raising and educating my daughter.

I learned about the benefits of using teaching strategies based on behavioral principles coupled with utilizing Sarah's strength-based modalities (like visual learning and imitative skills). Using these strategies, we could teach her appropriate behavior such as keeping her tongue in her mouth and preempt inappropriate behavior like biting. We could also teach her essential academic skills such as recognizing shapes and colors. This model was also inclusive, because it enabled children with disabilities to be educated alongside their typical peers. With the support of the families from the local organization, I learned about the research, strategies, and advocacy skills to enable individuals with Down syndrome and others with differing abilities to be appropriately included in their communities, and I was able to work closely with the early intervention program and the Committee on Preschool Special Education to create educational plans that kept Sarah in her community.

Sarah had home-based services that used applied behavior analysis and related services. We enrolled in a Mommy and Me program at a neighborhood school where she also attended preschool. In addition, Sarah attended the community recreational and dance programs and had playdates with neighborhood children. Itinerant special education teachers and related service providers came into the classroom to support Sarah and the professionals when needed. The at-home ABA program based on discrete trial teaching provided the targeted and scaffolded teaching supports that Sarah needed to learn. Sarah's participation in her neighborhood preschool enabled her to demonstrate mastery of skills learned in discrete trials, to benefit from interactions with peer models, and to form friendships with children in her community.

Sarah's special education teacher often relayed examples of how all the children benefitted from having Sarah in their class. For example, Sarah sometimes sucked her thumb, which her teacher corrected. Sarah's friend who was also sucking her thumb witnessed the teacher's correction and promptly took her thumb out of her mouth, saying that she would not do it either. This inclusive preschool experience in the least restrictive environment also enabled Sarah to transition into an inclusive kindergarten at the neighborhood school that her siblings attended rather than a more restrictive program in another school. Over a decade later, Sarah's educational team continues to work closely to create Individualized Educational Programs for her that are strength-based and exemplify the least restrictive environment.

As with all people, Sarah is the sum of her experiences. For example, if she is nurtured with language, physical activity, and peer interactions in developmentally appropriate ways, she is motivated to learn and achieve her personal best. At fifteen, Sarah loves to dance, sing, swim, ride her two-wheeler, and text her friends of all abilities to ask them to go out to lunch, get manicures, or go to the movies. She can verbally ask for help; she does not hug strangers or bite to express her anger. Sarah says she wants to work in an office and sing at the regional professional baseball team's stadium. I explain to her that it is very hard to sing at that stadium but that, if she continues to practice reading and singing, she might perform one day on her high school stage. I would rather she "shoot for the moon and land amongst the stars" than be the victim of the culture of low expectation.

I am thankful that IDEA and the Olmstead Act* are based on best practice and support people with disabilities in their communities. I'm also thankful that our government funds technical assistance centers to educate and support families and professionals in providing people with disabilities with appropriate supports and services in the least restrictive environment. I encourage parents to learn and to use the resources that are available to help achieve their vision for their children. I am also thankful for the gatekeepers in communities such as my local parent organization that are committed to the inclusion of all people and urge each of us to take what we learn and pay it forward to help support others. I believe every person desires to be seen for who he or she is as a unique multifaceted individual rather than to be identified by one defining characteristic like ethnicity or disability.

---

* The Olmstead Act was a ruling made on June 22, 1999, by the US Supreme Court that unjustified segregation of persons with disabilities constitutes discrimination in violation of Title II of the Americans with Disabilities Act. The court held that public entities must provide community-based services to people with disabilities.

Owen's Story

by Owen's Dad (Michael Kelly)

It is hard to believe that nineteen years have gone by. It seems like only yesterday we were in the hospital being told that our third son, Owen, had Down syndrome. His brother Thomas was three and a half, and his brother John was fourteen months. What a life changer! As can be expected, it came as a shock to us, but I must say, our families and friends were incredibly supportive, as were the medical professionals who were involved early on in Owen's life. As I look back, I realize how lucky we were to have such a great support system.

Owen had a rocky start due to a series of medical problems. Those challenges help put his life in perspective for us. Our concerns with the diagnosis disappeared when he was fighting for his life. So, once his medical needs were addressed, we started to think positively about our future. That is when my wife and I made two commitments to each other: we would provide Owen with every opportunity his brothers had, and we would not live our lives any differently because Owen had Down syndrome. Nineteen years later, these remain our commitments.

When Owen was first receiving early intervention services, we were relieved to learn he would have one therapist working with him, rather than several coming and going. With a busy household, the thought of having two, three, or four therapists coming and going from our home several times a week was overwhelming. We had a lead interventionist who provided direct services while the other professionals shared their expertise. Everyone worked out of a binder that had dividers for each skill that was being worked on. We all recorded Owen's progress in this binder.

We quickly realized how important writing down Owen's progress was to his future programming. It was so clear how behavior analysis enhanced his development, and we had documentation to show it. This allowed us to advocate for behavioral strategies in his next placement. For example, because we met with such success when Owen was very young, we advocated for a behavioral approach during his preschool years. He was so successful using discrete trial instruction that we made sure a portion of each day during his preschool years was set aside for this type of intensive instruction. It took place at a center-based program, where he was also enrolled in an integrated class for part of the day. Because it was important for Owen to have the same experiences as his brothers, he also attended his community preschool. This model worked so well that, with his progress information in hand, we were able to advocate for a similar program as he moved on to kindergarten.

Programs combining applied behavior analysis with access to his typical peers were and are so important for Owen. My family's understanding of behavioral principles was critical to address his problem behavior and also teach him new and important things. You see, Owen loved attention. He loved when we sang to him, he loved being picked up and tickled, and he loved when we cheered him on. He would sing and dance and do adorable things just to get our attention. But, at the same time, he would run from us, touch things in the house that he should not touch, and pull his little sister's hair (yes, three years after Owen was born, we had a beautiful daughter). My first instinct was to go to him, stop him from doing what he was doing, and then talk to him about it. And he was so darn cute that I would end up hugging him, tickling him, and then carrying him around on my shoulders right after.

When the behaviorists on our team observed us, they carefully explained how, when good things follow behaviors, those behaviors increase. Well, I'm a pretty quick learner myself, so once I realized that what I was doing increased those problem behaviors, I stopped reacting in that way. I just kept telling myself, "Catch Owen being good and then give him all of those hugs."

I know also that Owen has always succeeded in school because his school staff were well versed in dealing with problem behavior. Since preschool, we have had great plans in place for him. The token system is amazing. We used it both at home and school. And, we always had and still do have lots of pictures that show Owen what he should be doing. Also, our regular meetings with school staff enabled us to work together to solve problems before they got out of hand.

Applied behavior analysis really helped us with the challenges that we faced through Owen's toddler years. For example, he had a habit of only eating some foods. We are a family who loves to eat, and our other boys ate everything we cooked. No separate meals in this house. So, when Owen came along, it was really challenging for us, as he seemed to eat the same few things over and over again. At first, we started giving him those same foods. But we soon realized that was a problem when we were out and about. We also became concerned about his health, as cucumbers and meatballs do not make for a well-balanced diet. Our team soon came up with a great plan to address his eating: we kept his favorite food items in sight on a special plate when we presented the new food item, and we didn't take the new food item away when he said "no!" We also made a huge deal out of it when he did eat the new food. We cheered, gave him high fives, and sang his favorite songs.

I can't stress enough how well the simple strategies we learned worked with Owen, and they worked with our other children as well. I don't think I ever asked my children to do chores or to get dressed without giving them a choice!

We also realized that these same strategies could be used to teach Owen all sorts of things. Early on, we watched his teachers use discrete trial teaching and quickly learned to do it ourselves. When I say "we," I mean our entire family. We figured out what he needed to learn and then we gave him lots of opportunities right in a row to practice.

One area that has always been a particular concern for our family is Owen's ability to communicate. So, when we hear him say a word the wrong way or see that he is unable to answer someone's question or is not able to participate in a conversation or interaction because he doesn't have the words, we make it a priority to teach those things. For example, when he was about five years old, we realized he had difficulty with many of the words needed to play the card game "Go Fish." So, we used discrete trial teaching to teach him, "Do you have a…?" and each of the names of the cards (e.g., queen, king, jack, etc.). He soon became a champion "Go Fish" player. We did notice that Owen cheated a bit—his brothers swear he learned that on his own.

Another way we have all helped teach Owen is that we make sure that he knows how to say the names of his favorite foods so he can order when we eat out at restaurants. When he was little, we taught him to say things like *Sicilian pizza, vanilla milk shake,* and *chicken parmigiana.* Right now, we are working on pronouncing the names of new players on his favorite baseball team.

We not only use these strategies to teach Owen how to say things, but other skills as well. For example, things he needs to know to play sports, to make dance moves, and even to dress himself. His brothers and sister always knew that if Owen had lots of practice, he would eventually learn things, and they were so good at making sure it was fun for him. When he was young, a professional asked me, "What do you do when you play with the boys?" When I told her, she wrote down things that I could do while playing to help Owen follow up on the things that his teachers were working on in school. For example, we would play King of the Mountain (with me being the mountain) in the living room. The three boys would climb up on me, wrestling each other to be the only one on top. Well, there were so many goals that we could address in this game. We helped Owen say "My turn" when he wanted to go first and say "I won" when he was the only one on top. And I can remember as if it were yesterday teaching him to use his words and say "Stop that" instead of biting his brothers. I can also remember when he was learning to stand on one foot, I told all three of the boys to stand on one foot before they were allowed to start climbing on top of me. Teaching Owen things just became part of our everyday routine.

Owen's siblings, the kids in the neighborhood, and the kids at school have had a huge influence on him. Owen has always been around typical children. With Owen being such a good imitator, he tries to do everything that they do. I can remember bringing him to the library program when he was only two. He had been watching children's musical shows at home and imitating what he saw on TV. The library program had the same songs and actions, and Owen knew every move! He also imitated his classmates, which is why including him with typical students was so important. Also, we know that the key to Owen's success has been high expectations. We didn't, and still don't, want so many "special" things. That means he went on the big bus, went to the same schools as his brothers, played in the same sports leagues, learned to use the same type of cell phone, and did the same chores at home!

Now, there certainly have been a few obstacles along the way. We did lots of preparation with our district before his transition to kindergarten. We made it clear to everyone who would listen that it was our goal for Owen to attend the same school as his siblings and the other kids in the neighborhood. We had lots of meetings, and I spent lots of time on the phone sharing our dream. We were fortunate that the administrators in our school district agreed that Owen would benefit from being around his typical peers. They also saw the progress he made using intensive instruction and agreed with us that it was important to have his school staff well versed in strategies to address challenging behavior. With these things in place, we continued to use this model from preschool right through to where he is today, having a college experience at our local university—and we continue to fall back on our family's commitments. It has worked for Owen in the past, and we're pretty sure it will continue to work for him throughout his adulthood.

APPENDIX A
Program Sheets and Progress Trackers

Program Planner

Name: **Program:**

| Discrete trial teaching | Instruction embedded within an activity | Naturalistic instruction |

Materials:

S^D:

Target Skill:

Prompt:

Consequences:

    Correct response

    No response

    Incorrect response

Prompt Fading:

Planning for Generalization:

Criterion for Mastery:

Probing for Maintenance:

Progress Tracker – Discrete Trial Teaching

Name: **Program:**

Date	Target		Correct, Prompted, or Incorrect Response	% Correct	Caregiver

- Prompt:

Notes:

- Prompt:

Notes:

- Prompt:

Notes:

- Prompt:

Notes:

- Prompt:

Notes:

- Prompt:

Notes:

- Prompt:

Notes:

- Prompt:

Notes:

- Prompt:

Notes:

Progress Tracker – Instruction Embedded within an Activity

Name:

Activity:

| **Program:** | **Target:** | | **Program:** | **Target:** |

Learning Opportunity:

Learning Opportunity:

Date: _____ %

Date: _____ %

Date: _____ %

Date: _____ %

| **Program:** | **Target:** | | **Program:** | **Target:** |

Learning Opportunity:

Learning Opportunity:

Date: _____ %

Date: _____ %

Date: _____ %

Date: _____ %

Progress Tracker – Naturalistic Instruction

Name:　　　　　　　　　　　　　　　　　**Caregiver:**

Program:	Target:					Program:	Target:				
	Date:						Date:				
Learning Opportunity:		+	P	-		Learning Opportunity:		+	P	-	
		+	P	-				+	P	-	
		+	P	-				+	P	-	
		+	P	-				+	P	-	
		+	P	-				+	P	-	
		+	P	-				+	P	-	
		+	P	-				+	P	-	
		+	P	-				+	P	-	
		+	P	-				+	P	-	
		+	P	-				+	P	-	
Program:	Target:					Program:	Target:				
	Date:						Date:				
Learning Opportunity:		+	P	-		Learning Opportunity:		+	P	-	
		+	P	-				+	P	-	
		+	P	-				+	P	-	
		+	P	-				+	P	-	
		+	P	-				+	P	-	
		+	P	-				+	P	-	
		+	P	-				+	P	-	
		+	P	-				+	P	-	
		+	P	-				+	P	-	
		+	P	-				+	P	-	
Program:	Target:					Program:	Target:				
	Date:						Date:				
Learning Opportunity:		+	P	-		Learning Opportunity:		+	P	-	
		+	P	-				+	P	-	
		+	P	-				+	P	-	
		+	P	-				+	P	-	
		+	P	-				+	P	-	
		+	P	-				+	P	-	
		+	P	-				+	P	-	
		+	P	-				+	P	-	
		+	P	-				+	P	-	
		+	P	-				+	P	-	

Graph

Name:

Program:

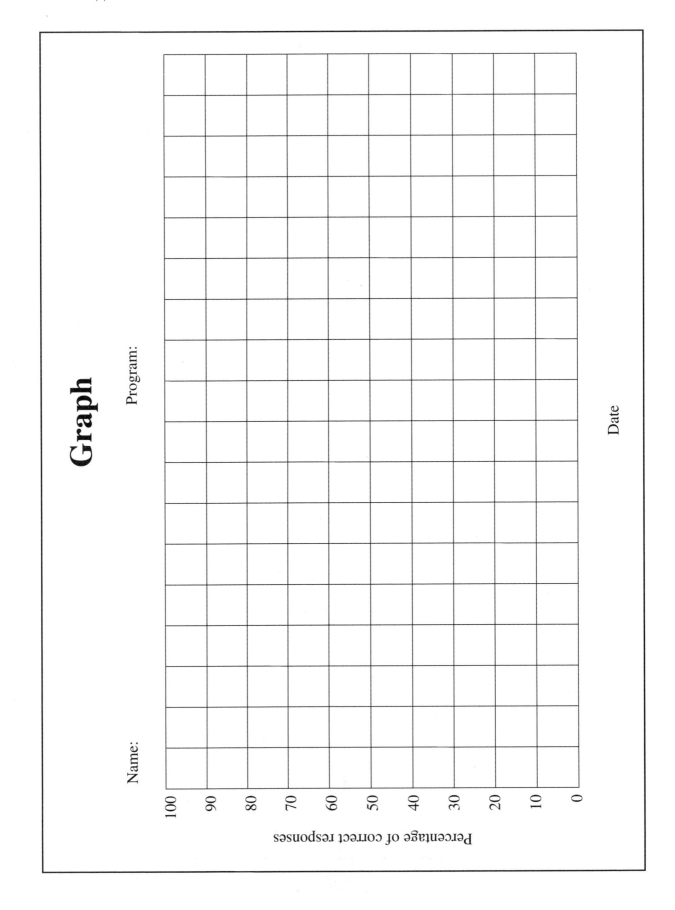

Percentage of correct responses

100 90 80 70 60 50 40 30 20 10 0

Date

APPENDIX B
Resources

Resources on Behavior Analysis, PBS, and Other Behavioral Issues

Organizations

American Psychological Association/Divisions
www.apa.org/about/division/

The American Psychological Association (APA) is the world's largest association of psychologists. The organization promotes research and disseminates findings through publications and conferences and establishes ethical standards for the field. APA has 56 divisions focused on specific topics. Division 25, the Behavior Analysis division, may be a useful resource for parents and professionals seeking information on applied behavior analysis.

Association for Behavior Analysis
www.abainternational.org

The Association for Behavior Analysis International (ABAI) is the primary membership organization for those interested in behavior analysis. Professionals can connect with each other via this association, and parents can connect with professionals by using ABAI to locate a behavior analyst to work with their child. Additional resources available through ABAI include journal publications and conferences and other educational events. There are also local affiliate chapters that may provide additional resources in your area.

Association for Positive Behavior Support
www.apbs.org

The Association for Positive Behavior Support focuses on research, policy, and networking regarding the use of positive behavior supports to improve quality of life for individuals with disabilities and their families. Through this organization, professionals and family members can network locally, access informative webinars and other informational materials, and find volunteer opportunities.

Association of Professional Behavior Analysts
www.apbahome.net

The Association of Professional Behavior Analysts is particularly useful for practitioners in the field of ABA, providing resources, education, and advocacy.

Behavior Analyst Certification Board
www.bacb.com

The Behavior Analyst Certification Board provides the certification credentials for behavior analysts. Professionals can use this resource to maintain credentials, while parents can use the online search function to locate behavior analysts and review their credentials.

Cambridge Center for Behavioral Studies
www.behavior.org

The Cambridge Center for Behavioral Studies disseminates information about behavior analysis through global collaboration and education. Publications, videos, podcasts, and continuing education opportunities are available on a number of topics in behavior analysis.

Positive Behavioral Interventions & Supports: OSEP Technical Assistance Center
www.pbis.org

The Technical Assistance Center on Positive Behavioral Interventions and Supports (PBIS) is part of the US Department of Education's Office of Special Education Programs (OSEP). The center works to help states, districts, and schools utilize PBIS. The Technical Assistance Center offers assistance to families and communities, including information on integrating PBIS into your family's everyday life. Questions can be e-mailed to tapbis@ku.edu.

Technical Assistance Center on Social Emotional Intervention for Young Children (TACSEI)
http://challengingbehavior.fmhi.usf.edu/index.htm

TACSEI supports caregivers and practitioners in using evidence-based practices with children with social-emotional needs. The website includes information, videos, and presentations about the Pyramid Model for Supporting Social-Emotional Competence (discussed in Book 2).

Books

Alberto, P. A., & Troutman, A. C. (2017). *Applied behavior analysis for teachers* (9th ed.). Upper Saddle River, NJ: Pearson.

Brown, F. E., McDonnell, J. J., & Snell, M. E. (2016). *Instruction of students with severe disabilities* (8th ed.). Upper Saddle River, NJ: Pearson.

Carr, E. G., Levin, L., McConachie, G., Carlson, J. I., Kemp, D. C., & Smith, C. E. (1994). *Communication-based intervention for problem behavior: A user's guide for producing positive change.* Baltimore, MD: Paul H. Brookes.

Clinical Practice Guideline: The Guideline Technical Report. Down syndrome, Assessment and Intervention for Young Children (Age 0–3 Years). New York State Department of Health, Division of Family Health Bureau of Early Intervention. Publication No. 4959. https://www.health.ny.gov/community/infants_children/early_intervention/memoranda.htm.

Cooper, J. O., Heron, T. E., & Heward, W. L. (2007). *Applied behavior analysis* (2nd ed.). Upper Saddle River, NJ: Pearson.

Dmitriev, V. (2001). *Time to begin: Early education for children with Down syndrome* (2nd ed.). Austin, TX: Pro-ed. (Out of print.)

Dunlap, G., Wilson, K., Strain, P.S., & Lee, J. K. (2013). *Prevent-teach-reinforce for young children: The early childhood model of individualized positive behavior support.* Baltimore, MD: Paul H. Brookes.

Hanson, M. J. (1987). *Teaching the infant with Down syndrome: A guide for parents and professionals* (2nd ed.). Austin, TX: Pro-ed. (Out of print.)

Heward, W. L., et al. (2005). *Focus on behavior analysis in education: Achievements, challenges, and opportunities.* Upper Saddle River, NJ: Pearson.

Johnston, S. S., Reichle, J., Feeley, K. M., & Jones, E. A. (2012). *AAC strategies for individuals with moderate to severe disabilities.* Baltimore, MD: Paul H. Brookes.

Lovaas, O. I. (1987). *Teaching developmentally disabled children: The ME book.* Austin, TX: Pro-ed. (Out of print.)

Maurice, C., Green, G., & Luce, S. C. (Eds.) (1996). *Behavioral intervention for young children with autism: A manual for parents and professionals.* Austin, TX: Pro-ed.

Maurice, C., Green, G., & Foxx, R. M. (Eds.) (2001). *Making a difference: Behavioral intervention for autism.* Austin, TX: Pro-ed.

Mayer, G.R., Sulzer-Azaroff, B., & Wallace, M. (2013). *Behavior analysis for lasting change* (3rd ed.). Cornwall-on-Hudson, NY: Sloan.

O'Neill, R. E., Albin, R. W., Storey, K., Horner, R. H., & Sprague, J. R. (2015). *Functional assessment and program development for problem behavior: A practical handbook* (3rd ed.). Independence, KY: Cengage Learning.

Reichle, J. E., & Wacker, D. (2017). *Functional communication training for problem behavior.* New York, NY: Guilford Press.

Stein, D. S. (2016). *Supporting positive behavior in children and teens with Down syndrome: The respond but don't react method.* Bethesda, MD: Woodbine House.

Journals

Some journals listed below focus heavily on studies of applied behavior analysis (e.g., *Journal of Applied Behavior Analysis)*, while others publish a wider range of studies of interventions and more descriptive research about the needs of individuals with disabilities (e.g., *Research in Developmental Disabilities*).

American Journal of Intellectual and Developmental Disabilities
(formerly called *American Journal on Mental Retardation* and *American Journal on Mental Deficiency*)
http://www.aaiddjournals.org/

Applied Research in Mental Retardation
(incorporated into *Research in Developmental Disabilities*)
http://www.sciencedirect.com/science/journal/02703092

Augmentative and Alternative Communication
https://www.isaac-online.org/english/publications/aac/

Behavior Analysis: Research and Practice
http://www.apa.org/pubs/journals/bar/index.aspx

Behavioral Interventions
http://onlinelibrary.wiley.com/journal/10.1002/(ISSN)1099-078X

Behavior Modification
http://bmo.sagepub.com/

Down Syndrome Research and Practice
https://www.down-syndrome.org/research-practice/

Education and Training in Autism and Developmental Disabilities http://www.daddcec.org/Publications/ETADDJournal.aspx

Journal of Applied Behavior Analysis
http://onlinelibrary.wiley.com/journal/10.1002/(ISSN)1938-3703

Journal of Developmental and Physical Disabilities
https://link.springer.com/journal/10882

Journal of Positive Behavioral Interventions
http://pbi.sagepub.com/

Research in Developmental Disabilities
http://www.journals.elsevier.com/research-in-developmental-disabilities/

Other Helpful Resources

Down Syndrome

National Down Syndrome Congress
www.ndsccenter.org/
800-232-6372

The National Down Syndrome Congress (NDSC) is a resource for advocacy, public awareness, and information for individuals with Down syndrome and their families. NSDC provides access to articles, local and national support, and conferences.

National Down Syndrome Association
www.ndss.org/
800-221-4602
Through parent resources, a helpline, and a variety of initiatives and programs, the National Down Syndrome Society (NDSS) works to improve the value, acceptance, and inclusion of individuals with Down syndrome.

Down Syndrome Education International
www.dseinternational.org/en-us/
https://store.dseusa.org/
Through research, services, and a variety of educational programs, Down Syndrome Education International seeks to improve educational outcomes for children with Down syndrome. A variety of teaching materials and publications for parents and professionals are available.

Down Syndrome Medical Guidelines
http://pediatrics.aappublications.org/content/128/2/393
These guidelines are for pediatricians who care for children with Down syndrome and their families.

Inclusion

Best Buddies
http://bestbuddies.org/
305-374-2233 (toll free)
Through one-to-one friendships, integrated employment, and leadership development, Best Buddies International helps individuals with intellectual and developmental disabilities be integrated into their schools and communities. Through the website, parents can find local Best Buddies chapters, donate, volunteer, and view upcoming events or walks.

National Professional Development Center on Inclusion
http://npdci.fpg.unc.edu
This national center works with states to ensure early childhood teachers are prepared to educate and care for young children with disabilities in settings with their typically developing peers. It provides forums for parents and professionals to share challenges, ask questions, and contribute ideas on issues related to early childhood professional development and inclusion.

National Center on Health, Physical Activity and Disability
www.nchpad.org
800-900-8086

The National Center on Health, Physical Activity and Disability (NCHPAD) provides resources to promote participation in physical and social activities for individuals with disabilities.

Swift: Schoolwide Integrated Framework for Transformation
www.swiftschools.org/

SWIFT is a national K-8 technical assistance center to help schools provide academic and behavior support to ensure all students are welcome and included in age-appropriate general education classrooms. The website offers a library of research and resources pertaining to the program and schools that use it.

Intellectual and Developmental Disabilities

American Association on Intellectual and Developmental Disabilities
www.aaidd.org

The AAIDD is a professional organization concerned with improving the quality of life for individuals with intellectual disabilities through conferences, continuing education, networking, and publications. The website offers resources that can help parents and professionals obtain helpful information when caring for an individual with an intellectual or developmental disability.

Parent to Parent USA
www.p2pusa.org
855-238-8979

Parent to Parent provides emotional and information support for families of children with special needs by matching an experienced support parent to families in need.

Laws and Advocacy

Council of Parent Attorneys and Advocates
www.copaa.org/?SEAT

Council of Parent Attorneys and Advocates (COPAA) is a group of attorneys, advocates, parents, and other professionals working to protect the legal and civil rights of students with disabilities.

Individuals with Disabilities Education Act
http://idea.ed.gov
https://sites.ed.gov/idea/
    The Individuals with Disabilities Education Act of 2004 (IDEA) is the law governing how states provide to children with disabilities in the United States.

National Association for Professional Education Advocates
http://www.napsea.co/
    NAPSEA provides families and professionals with resources, information, professional development, and networking, to increase knowledge and promote the rights of children and young adults with disabilities.

National Legal Aid & Defender Association (NLADA)
http://www.nlada100years.org/
    NLADA is devoted to delivering legal services to those who cannot afford counsel. NLADA provides advocacy, information, and training to members of the equal justice community. Families can use this resource for human rights information, view available resources, and seek proper advocacy for loved ones with disabilities.

Office of Special Education and Rehabilitative Services
http://www2.ed.gov/about/offices/list/osers/index.html
202-245-7459
    OSERS is the office of the US Department of Education that oversees special education and rehabilitative services. Through research and state grants and technical assistance centers, OSERS works to improve outcomes for people with disabilities.

Partners in Policy
www.mn.gov/mnddc/pop/mclassroom.html
    Operating in many states, Partners in Policy is a training program for individuals with disabilities or family members who wish to be a voice for all individuals with disabilities.

Wrightslaw
http://wrightslaw.com/
    Wrightslaw provides extensive information and training for parents, educators, advocates, and attorneys about special education law, education law, and advocacy for children with disabilities.

Mealtime and Oral Motor Skills

Flag House
www.flaghouse.com and www.especialneeds.com
   Both websites provide useful information and materials for purchase related to a range of needs, including adaptive utensils and other adaptive equipment.

Pediatric Feeding News
www.pediatricfeedingnews.com
   This is a very user-friendly web resource that addresses many issues related to feeding.

TalkTools
www.talktools.com
   Rosenfeld-Johnson's horns, whistles, and straws.

Thick-It
www.thickit.com
   The company offers a powder that can be used to thicken liquids.

Miscellaneous

Bob Books
bobbooks.com/

ICanRead!
https://www.icanread.com/levels

Watch Me Learn
www.watchmelearn.com/and https://www.youtube.com/c/watchmelearn/videos

REFERENCES

This is a list of publications related to the Down syndrome behavioral phenotype and interventions for children with Down syndrome. The bibliography for articles demonstrating the effectiveness of applied behavior analytic interventions with individuals with Down syndrome is at the end of Chapter 2 in this book. Resources about behavior analysis, Down syndrome, the law, etc. are referenced in Appendix B.

Abbeduto, L., Murphy, M. M., Cawthon, S. W., Richmond, E. K., Weissman, M. D., Karadottir, S., & O'Brien, A. (2003). Receptive language skills of adolescents and young adults with Down or fragile X syndrome. *American Journal on Mental Retardation, 108* (3), 149–160.

Aumonier, M. E., & Cunningham, C. C. (1983). Breast feeding in infants with Down's syndrome. *Child: Care, Health, and Development, 9*, 247–255.

Avant, M. J. T., & Heller, K. W. (2011). Examining the effectiveness of TouchMath with students with physical disabilities. *Remedial and Special Education, 32* (4), 309–321. doi: 10.1177/0741932510362198

Baddeley, A., & Jarrold, C. (2007). Working memory and Down syndrome. *Journal of Intellectual Disability Research, 51* (12), 925–931. doi: 10.1111/j.1365-2788.2007.00979.x

Bauer, S., & Jones, E. A. (2014). A behavior analytic approach to exploratory motor (EM) behavior: How can caregivers teach EM behavior to infants with Down syndrome? *Infants and Young Children, 27* (2), 161–172. doi: 10.1097/IYC.0000000000000004

Bauer, S., & Jones, E. A. (2015). Requesting and verbal imitation intervention for infants with Down syndrome: Generalization, intelligibility, and problem solving. *Journal of Developmental and Physical Disabilities, 27*, 37–66. doi: 10.1007/s10882-014-9400-6

Baylis, P., & Snowling, M. J. (2011). Evaluation of a phonological reading programme for children with Down syndrome. *Child Language Teaching and Therapy, 28* (1), 39–56. doi: 10.1177/0265659011414277

Becker, W., & Engelmann, S. (1973). *Program description and 1973 outcome data: Englemann-Becker follow through model.* Washington, DC: Bureau of Elementary and Secondary Education, Division of Compensatory Education.

Becker, D. R., Miao, A., Duncan, R., & McClelland, M. M. (2014). Behavioral self-regulation and executive function both predict visuomotor skills and early academic achievement. *Early Childhood Research Quarterly, 29,* 411–424. http://dx.doi.org/10.1016/j.ecresq.2014.04.014

Belacchi, C., Passolunghi, M. C., Brentan, E., Dante, A., Persi, L., & Cornoldi, C. (2014). Approximate additions and working memory in individuals with Down syndrome. *Research in Developmental Disabilities, 35,* 1027–1035. http://dx.doi.org/10.1016/j.ridd.2014.01.036

Berry, P., Gunn, P., & Andrews, R. J. (1984). The behavior of Down's syndrome children using the 'lock box': A research note. *Journal of Child Psychology and Psychiatry, 25* (1), 125–131.

Betz, A. M., Higbee, T. S., Kelley, K. N., Sellers, T. P., & Pollard, J. S. (2011). Increasing response variability of mand frames with script training and extinction. *Journal of Applied Behavior Analysis, 44* (2), 357–362. doi: 10.1901/jaba.2011.44-357

Bidder, R. T., Bryant, G., & Gray, O. P. (1975). Benefits to Down's syndrome children through training their mothers. *Archives of Disease in Childhood, 50,* 383-386.

Bierman, K. L., Nix, R. L., Greenberg, M. T., Blair, C., & Domitrovich, C. E. (2008). Executive functions and school readiness intervention: Impact, moderation, and mediation in the Head Start REDI program. *Development and Psychopathology, 20,* 821–843. doi:10.1017/S0954579408000394

Binder, C., & Watkins, C. L. (1990). Precision teaching and Direct instruction: Measurably superior instructional technology in schools. *Performance Improvement Quarterly, 3* (4), 74–96. doi: 10.1111/j.1937-8327.1990.tb00478.x

Boberg, E., & Fong, L. (1980). Therapy program for young retarded stutterers. *Human Communication, Summer,* 94–102.

Borella, E., Carretti, B., & Lanfranchi, S. (2013). Inhibitory mechanisms in Down syndrome: Is there a specific or general deficit. *Research in Developmental Disabilities, 34,* 65–71. http://dx.doi.org/10.1016/j.ridd.2012.07.017

Bradley-Johnson, S., Friedrich, D. D., & Wyrembelski, A. R. (1981). Exploratory behavior in Down's syndrome and normal infants. *Applied Research in Mental Retardation, 2,* 213–228.

Bray, M. (2003). The nature of dysfluency in Down's syndrome. Retrieved from http://www.stammering.org/speaking-out/articles/nature-dysfluency-downs-syndrome

Brock, J., & Jarrold, C. (2004). Language influences on verbal short-term memory performance in Down syndrome: Item and order recognition. *Journal of Speech, Language, and Hearing Research, 47,* 1334–1346.

Bruce, S., Campbell, C., & Sullivan, M. (2009). Supporting children with severe disabilities to achieve means-end. *TEACHING Exceptional Children Plus, 6* (1), Article 2. Retrieved from http://escholarship.bc.edu/education/tecplus/vol6/iss1/art2

Bruce, S., & Muhammad, Z. (2009). The development of object permanence in children with intellectual disability, physical disability, autism, and blindness. *International Journal of Disability, Development and Education, 56* (3), 229–246. doi: 10.1080/10349120903102213

Bruni, M. (2016). *Fine motor skills for children with Down syndrome: A guide for parents and professionals* (3rd ed.). Bethesda, MD: Woodbine House.

Buckley, S. J., Bird, G., & Sacks, B. (2006). Evidence that we can change the profile from a study of inclusive education. *Down Syndrome Research and Practice, 9* (3), 51–53.

Buckley, S. J., Bird, G., Sacks, B., & Archer, T. (2006). A comparison of mainstream and special education for teenagers with Down syndrome: Implications for parents and teachers. *Down Syndrome Research and Practice, 9* (3), 54–67.

Burgoyne, K., Duff, F. J., Clarke, P. J., Buckley, S., Snowling, M. J., & Hulme, C. (2012). Efficacy of a reading and language intervention for children with Down syndrome: A randomized controlled trial. *Journal of Child Psychology and Psychiatry, 53* (10), 1044–1053. doi:10.1111/j.1469-7610.2012.02557.x

Cameron, C. E., Brock, L. L., Murrah, W. M., Bell, L. H., Worzalla, S. L., Grissmer, D., & Morrison, F. J. (2012). Fine motor skills and executive function both contribute to kindergarten achievement. *Child Development, 83* (4), 1229–1244. doi: 10.1111/j.1467-8624.2012.01768.x

Cammilleri, A. P., & Hanley, G. P. (2005). Use of a lag differential reinforcement contingency to increase varied selections of classroom activities. *Journal of Applied Behavior Analysis, 38* (1), 111–115. doi: 10.1901/jaba.2005.34-04

Carney, D. J., Brown, J. H., & Henry, L. A. (2013). Executive function in Williams and Down syndromes. *Research in Developmental Disabilities, 34,* 46–55. http://dx.doi.org/10.1016/j.ridd.2012.07.013

Carney, D. P. J., Henry, L. A., Messer, D. J., Danielsson, H., Brown, J. H., & Rönnberg, J. (2013). Using developmental trajectories to examine verbal and visuospatial short-term memory development in children and adolescents with Williams and Down syndromes. *Research in Developmental Disabilities, 34,* 3421–3432. http://dx.doi.org/10.1016/j.ridd.2013.07.012

Chapman, R. S., & Hesketh, L. J. (2000). Behavioral phenotype of individuals with Down syndrome. *Mental Retardation and Developmental Disabilities Research Reviews, 6,* 84–95.

Chapman, R. S., Seung, H., Schwartz, S. E., & Kay-Raining Bird, E. (1998). Language skills of children and adolescents with Down syndrome: II. Production deficits. *Journal of Speech, Language, and Hearing Research, 41,* 861–873.

Chen, C., Ringenbach, S. D. R., Albert, A., & Semken, K. (2014). Fine motor control is related to cognitive control in adolescents with Down syndrome. *International Journal of Disability, Development and Education, 61* (1), 6–15. doi: 10.1080/1034912X.2014.878532

Chiesa, M., & Robertson, A. (2000). Precision teaching and fluency training: Making maths easier for pupils and teachers. *Educational Psychology in Practice, 16* (3), 297–310.

Clinical Practice Guidelines: Report of the Recommendations: Down Syndrome for Young Children (Age 0-3 Years) (2006). New York State Department of Health Early Intervention Program.

Clunies-Ross, G. G. (1979). Accelerating the development of Down's syndrome infants and young children. *The Journal of Special Education, 13* (2), 169-177.

Condeluci, A. (2015). *Social Capital: The Key to Macro Change.* Youngville, NC: Lash and Associates Publishing/Training, Inc.

Connor, F. P. Williamson, G. G., & Siepp, J. M. (Eds.) (1978). *Program Guide for Infants and Toddlers with Neuromotor and Other Developmental Disabilities.* New York: Teachers College Press.

Contestabile, A., Benfenati, F., & Gasparini, L. (2010). Communication breaks down: From neurodevelopment defects to cognitive disabilities in Down syndrome. *Progress in Neurobiology, 91,* 1–22. doi:10.1016/j.pneurobio.2010.01.003

Costanzo, F., Varuzza, C., Menghini, D., Addona, F., Gianesini, T., & Vicari, S. (2013). Executive functions in intellectual disabilities: A comparison between Williams syndrome and Down syndrome. *Research in Developmental Disabilities, 34,* 1770–1780. http://dx.doi.org/10.1016/j.ridd.2013.01.024

Couzens, D., Haynes, M., & Cuskelly, M. (2012). Individual and environmental characteristics associated with cognitive development in Down syndrome: A longitudinal study. *Journal of Applied Research in Intellectual Disabilities, 25,* 396–413.

Critchfield, T. S., & Fienup, D. (2008). Stimulus equivalence. In S. F. Davis, & W. Buskist (Eds.). *21st Century Psychology: A Reference Handbook* (pp. 360–372). Thousand Oaks, CA: Sage.

Dale, P. S., & Hayden, D. A. (2013). Treating speech subsystems in childhood apraxia of speech with tactual input: The PROMPT approach. *American Journal of Speech-Language Pathology, 22* (4), 644–661. doi: 10.1044/1058-0360(2013/12-0055)

Daunhauer, L. A., Fidler, D. J., Hahn, L., Will, E., Lee, N. R., & Hepburn, S. (2014). Profiles of everyday executive functioning in young children with Down syndrome. *American Journal on Intellectual and Developmental Disabilities, 119* (4), 303–318. doi: 10.1352/1944–7558-119.4.303

Davis, A. S. (2008). Children with Down syndrome: Implications for assessment and intervention in the school. *School Psychology Quarterly, 23* (2), 271–281. doi: 10.1037/1045-3830.23.2.271

Davis, W. E., Sparrow, W. A., & Ward, T. (1991). Fractionated reaction times and movement times of Down syndrome and other adults with mental retardation. *Adapted Physical Activity Quarterly, 8,* 221–233.

Davis, B., & Velleman, S. (2000). Differential diagnosis and treatment of developmental apraxia of speech in infants and toddlers. *Infant-Toddler Intervention, 10,* 177–192.

De Graaf, G., Van Hove, G., & Haveman, M. (2012). Effects of regular versus special school placement on students with Down syndrome: A systematic review of studies. In A. van den Bosch and E. Dubois (Eds.). *New Developments in Down Syndrome Research* (pp. 45–86). Hauppauge, NY: Nova Science Publishers.

De Graaf, G., Van Hove, G., & Haveman, M. (2013). A quantitative assessment of educational integration of students with Down syndrome in the Netherlands. *Journal of Intellectual Disability Research, 58* (7), 1–12. doi:10.1111.jir.12060

De Graaf, G., Van Hove, G., & Haveman, M. (2013). More academics in regular schools? The effect of regular versus special school placement on academic skills in Dutch primary school students with Down syndrome. *Journal of Intellectual Disability Research, 57* (1), 21–38. doi:10.111.j.1365-2788.2011.01512.x

Devenny, D. A., & Silverman, W. P. (1990). Speech dysfluency and manual specialization in Down's syndrome. *Journal of Mental Deficiency Research, 34,* 253–260.

Drash, P. W., Raver, S.A., Murrin, M.R., & Tudor, R. M. (1989). Three procedures for increasing vocal response to therapist prompt in infants and children with Down syndrome. *American Journal on Mental Retardation, 94,* 64-73.

Dunst, C. J. (1980). *A clinical and educational manual for use with the Uzgiris and Hunt Scales of Infant Psychological Development.* Austin, TX: Pro-Ed.

Dunst, C. J. (1988). Stage transitioning in the sensorimotor development of Down's syndrome infants. *Journal of Mental Deficiency Research, 32,* 405–410.

Dunst, C. J., & Rheingrover, R. M. (1983). Structural characteristics of sensorimotor development among Down's syndrome infants. *Journal of Mental Deficiency Research, 27,* 11–22.

Durand, V. M. (2014). *Sleep better! A guide to improving sleep for children with special needs* (revised ed.). Baltimore, MD: Brookes.

Durand, M. & Crimmins, D. B. (1992). *The motivation assessment scale administration guide.* Topeka, KS: Monaco & Associates.

Dyer, K., Dunlap, G., & Winterling, V. (1990). Effects of choice making on the serious problem behavior of students with severe handicaps. *Journal of Applied Behavior Analysis, 23* (4), 515–524.

Dykens, E. M. (1995). Measuring behavioral phenotypes: Provocations from the "new genetics." *American Journal on Mental Retardation, 99,* 522-532.

Eadie, P. A., Fey, M. E., Douglas, J. M., & Parsons, C. L. (2002). Profiles of grammatical morphology and sentence imitation in children with specific language impairment and Down syndrome. *Journal of Speech, Language, and Hearing Research, 45,* 720–732.

Edgin, J. O. (2013). Cognition in Down syndrome: A developmental cognitive neuroscience perspective. *WIREs Cognitive Science, 4,* 307–317. oi: 10.1002/wcs.1221

Faragher, R., & Clarke, B (Eds.) (2014). *Educating learners with Down syndrome: Research, theory, and practice with children and adolescents.* London: Routledge.

Feeley, K. M., Jones, E. A., Blackburn, C., & Bauer, S. (2011). Advancing imitation and requesting skills in toddlers with Down syndrome. *Research in Developmental Disabilities, 32,* 2415-2430. doi:10.1016/j.ridd.2011.07.018

Fey, M. E., Warren, S. F., Brady, N., Finestack. L. H., Bredin-Oja, S. L., Fairchild, M., Sokol, S., & Yoder, P. J. (2006). Early effects of responsivity education/prelinguistic milieu teaching for children with developmental delays and their parents. *Journal of Speech, Language, and Hearing Research, 49,* 526–547.

Fidler, D. J. (2005). The emerging Down syndrome behavioral phenotype in early childhood: Implications for practice. *Infants & Young Children, 18* (2), 86–103.

Fidler, D. J. (2006). The emergence of a syndrome-specific personality profile in young children with Down syndrome. *Down Syndrome Research and Practice, 10* (2), 53–60. doi:10.3104/reprints.305

Fidler, D. J. (2009). Early intervention in Down syndrome: Targeting the emerging behavioral phenotype. *Perspectives on Language Learning and Education, 16,* 83–89. doi:10.1044/lle16.3.83

Fidler, D. J., Hepburn, S. L., Mankin, G., & Rogers, S. J. (2005). Praxis skills in young children with Down syndrome, other developmental disabilities, and typically developing children. *The American Journal of Occupational Therapy, 59* (2), 129–138.

Fidler, D., Hepburn, S. L., & Osaki, D. (2011). Goal-directedness as a target for early intervention in Down syndrome. In J. A. Rondal, J. Perera, & D. Spiker (Eds.), *Neurocognitive rehabilitation of Down syndrome: Early years* (pp. 191–204). Cambridge, New York: Cambridge University Press.

Fidler, D. J., Hepburn, S. L., & Rogers, S. J. (2005). Early learning and adaptive behavior in toddlers with Down syndrome: Evidence for an emerging behavioural phenotype? *Down Syndrome Research and Practice, 9* (3), 37–44.

Fidler, D. J., Most, D. E., Booth-LaForce, C., & Kelly, J. F. (2006). Temperament and behaviour problems in young children with Down syndrome at 12, 30, and 45 months. *Down Syndrome Research and Practice, 10* (1), 23–29.

Fidler, D. J., Most, D. E., Booth-LaForce, C., & Kelly, J. F. (2008). Emerging social strengths in young children with Down syndrome. *Infants & Young Children, 21* (3), 207–220.

Fidler, D. J., Most, D. E., & Guiberson, M. M. (2005). Neuropsychological correlates of word identification in Down syndrome. *Research in Developmental Disabilities, 26,* 487–501. doi:10.1016/j.ridd.2004.11.007

Fidler, D. J., Most, D. E., & Philofsky, A. D. (2008). The Down syndrome behavioural phenotype: Taking a developmental approach. D*own Syndrome Research and Practice,* Advance online publication. doi:10.3104/reviews/2069

Fidler, D. J., & Nadell, L. (2007). Education and children with Down syndrome: Neuroscience, development, and intervention. *Mental Retardation and Developmental Disabilities Research Reviews, 13,* 262–271. doi: 10.1002/mrdd.20166

Fidler, D. J., Philofsky, A., & Hepburn, S. L. (2007). Language phenotypes and intervention planning: Bridging research and practice. *Mental Retardation and Developmental Disabilities Research Reviews, 13,* 47–57. doi: 10.1002/mrdd.20132

Fidler, D. J., Philofsky, A., Hepburn, S. L., & Rogers, S. (2005). Nonverbal requesting and problem-solving by toddlers with Down syndrome. *American Journal on Mental Retardation, 110* (4), 312–322.

Fidler, D. J., Will, E., Daunhauer, L. A., Gerlach-McDonald, B., & Visootsak, J. (2014). Object-related generativity in children with Down syndrome. *Research in Developmental Disabilities, 35,* 3379–3385. http://dx.doi.org/10.1016/j.ridd.2014.07.024 0891–4222/ _ 2014

Fiocca, S. (2007). *Oral motor and feeding skills.* Retrieved from http://www.riverbendds.org/index.htm?page=fiocca.html

Fletcher, D., Boon, R. T., & Cihak, D. F. (2010). Effects of the TOUCHMATH program compared to a number line strategy to teach addition facts to middle school students with moderate intellectual disabilities. *Education and Training in Autism and Developmental Disabilities, 45* (3), 449–458.

Fowler, A. E., Gelman, R., & Gleitman, L. R. (1994). The course of language learning in children with Down syndrome. In H. Tager-Flusberg (Ed.). *Constraints on language acquisition: Studies of atypical children* (pp. 91–140). Hillsdale, NJ: Lawrence Erlbaum Associates.

Frank, K., & Esvensen, A. J. (2015). Fine motor and self-care milestones for individuals with Down syndrome using a retrospective chart review. *Journal of Intellectual Disability Research, 59* (8), 719–729. doi: 10.1111/jir.12176

Froehlke, M., & Zaborek, R. (2013). *When Down Syndrome and Autism Intersect: A Guide to DS-ASD for Parents and Professionals.* Woodbine House: Bethesda, MD.

Goldstein, H. (1983). Recombinative generalization: Relationships between environmental conditions and the linguistic repertoires of language learners. *Analysis and Intervention in Developmental Disabilities, 3,* 279–293.

Goldstein, H. (1983). Training generative repertoires within agent-action-object miniature linguistic systems with children. *Journal of Speech and Hearing Research, 26,* 76–89.

Goldstein, H., Angelo, D., & Mousetis, L. (1987). Acquisition and extension of syntactic repertoires by severely mentally retarded youth. *Research in Developmental Disabilities, 8,* 549–574.

Gunn, D. M., & Jarrold, C. (2004). Raven's matrices performance in Down syndrome: Evidence of unusual errors. *Research in Developmental Disabilities, 25,* 443–457. doi:10.1016/j. ridd.2003.07.004

Hahn, L. J., Fidler, D. J., Hepburn, S. L., & Rogers, S. J. (2013). Early intersubjective skills and the understanding of intentionality in young children with Down syndrome. *Research in Developmental Disabilities, 34,* 4455–4465. http://dx.doi.org/10.1016/j.ridd.2013.09.027

Hanna, E. S., Kohlsdorf, M., Quinteiro, R. S., de Melo, R. M., de Souza, D. G., de Rose, J. C., & McIlvane, W. J. (2011). Recombinative reading derived from pseudoword instruction in a miniature linguistic system. *Journal of the Experimental Analysis of Behavior, 95* (1), 21–40. doi: 10.1901/jeab.2011.95-21

Hanson, M. J. (2003). Twenty-five years after early intervention: A follow-up of children with Down syndrome and their families. *Infants and Young Children, 16* (4), 354–365.

Hanson, M. J., & Schwarz, R. H. (1978). Results of a longitudinal intervention program for Down's syndrome infants and their families. *Education and Training of the Mentally Retarded, 13* (4), 403–407.

Harasym, J., & Langevin, M. (2012). Stuttering treatment for a school-aged child with Down syndrome: A descriptive case report. *Journal of Fluency Disorders, 37,* 253–262. http://dx.doi.org/101016.j.fludis.2012.01.002

Hauser-Cram, P., Woodman, A. C., & Heyman, M. (2014). Early mastery motivation as a predictor of executive function in young adults with developmental disabilities. *American Journal on Intellectual and Developmental Disabilities, 119* (6), 536–551. doi: 10. 1352/1944-7588-119.6.536

Henderson, S. E., Illingworth, S. M., & Allen, J. (1991). Prolongation of simple manual and vocal reaction times in Down syndrome. *Adapted Physical Activity Quarterly, 8,* 234–241.

Herrera, A. N., Bruno, A., Gonzalez, C., Moreno, L., & Sanabria, H. (2011). Addition and subtraction by students with Down syndrome. *International Journal of Mathematical Education in Science and Technology, 42* (1), 13–35. doi: 10.1080/0020739X.2010.500698

Heyman, M., & Hauser-Cram, P. (2015). Negative life events predict performance on an executive function task in young adults with developmental disabilities. *Journal of Intellectual Disability Research, 59* (8), 746–754. doi: 10.1111/jir.12181

Hodapp, R. M., & Fidler, D. J. (1999). Special education and genetics: Connections for the 21st century. *The Journal of Special Education, 33* (3), 130–137.

Hodapp, R. M., Leckman, J. F., Dykens, E. M., Sparrow, S. S., Zelinsky, D. G., & Ort, S. I. (1992). K-ABC profiles in children with fragile X syndrome, Down syndrome, and nonspecific mental retardation. *American Journal on Mental Retardation, 97* (1), 39–46.

Hodges, N. J., Cunningham, S. J., Lyons, J., Kerr, T. L., & Elliott, D. (1995). Visual feedback processing and goal-directed movement in adults with Down syndrome. *Adapted Physical Activity Quarterly, 12,* 176–186.

Horsler, K., & Oliver, C. (2006). Environmental influences on the behavioral phenotype of Angelman syndrome. *American Journal on Mental Retardation, 111,* 311–321.

Horstmeier, D. (2016). *Teaching Math to People with Down Syndrome and Other Hands-On Learners.* Bethesda, MD: Woodbine House.

Hulme, C., Goetz, K., Brigstocke, S., Nash, H. M., Lervag, A., & Snowling, M. J. (2012). The growth of reading skills in children with Down syndrome. *Developmental Science, 15* (3), 320–329. doi: 10.1111/j.1467-7687.2011.01129.x

Jarrold, C., & Baddeley, A. D. (1997). Short-term memory for verbal and visuospatial information in Down's syndrome. *Cognitive Neuropsychiatry, 2* (2), 101–122.

Jarrold, C., & Baddeley, A. D. (2001). Short-term memory in Down syndrome: Applying the working memory model. *Down Syndrome Research and Practice, 7* (1), 17–23.

Jarrold, C., Baddeley, A. D., & Hewes, A. (2000). Verbal short-term memory deficits in Down syndrome: A consequence of problems in rehearsal? *Journal of Child Psychology and Psychiatry, 40* (2), 233–244.

Jarrold, C., Baddeley, A. D., & Philips, C. E. (2002). Verbal short-term memory in Down syndrome: A problem of memory, audition, or speech? *Journal of Speech, Language, and Hearing Research, 45,* 531–544.

Jarrold, C., Cowan, N., Hewes, A. K., & Riby, D. M. (2004). Speech timing and verbal short-term memory: Evidence for contrasting deficits in Down syndrome and Williams syndrome. *Journal of Memory and Language, 51,* 365–380. doi:10.1016/j.jml.2004.06.007

Jarrold, C., Thron, A. S. C., & Stephens, E. (2009). The relationships among verbal short-term memory, phonological awareness, and new word learning: Evidence from typical development and Down syndrome. *Journal of Experimental Child Psychology, 102,* 196–218. doi:10.1016/j.jecp.2008.07.001

Jiar, Y. K., Xi, L., Satria, H., Zainiyah, S., & Yahya, S. (2012). Strength and weaknesses of children with Down syndrome (0–60 months) and comparison with typically developing children. *International Journal of Education and Information Technologies, 6* (2), 233–240.

Johnston, F., & Stansfield, J. (1997). Expressive pragmatic skills in pre-school children with and without Down's syndrome: Parental perceptions. *Journal of Intellectual Disability Research, 41* (1), 19–29.

Jones, E. A., Feeley, K. M., & Blackburn, C. (2010). A preliminary study of intervention addressing early developing requesting behaviours in young infants with Down syndrome. *Down Syndrome Research and Practice, 12* (3), 155–164. doi:10.3104/reports.2059

Joyce, B. G., & Wolking, W. D. (1989). Stimulus equivalence: An approach for teaching beginning reading skills to young children. *Education and Treatment of Children, 12* (2), 109–122.

Karaaslan, O., & Mahoney G. (2013). Effectiveness of responsive teaching with children with Down syndrome. *Intellectual and Developmental Disabilities, 51* (6), 458–469. doi: 10.1352/1934-9556-51.6.458

Kasari, C., & Freeman, S. F. N. (2001). Task-related social behavior in children with Down syndrome. *American Journal on Mental Retardation, 106* (3), 253–264.

Kent, R. D., & Vorperian, H. K. (2013). Speech impairment in Down syndrome: A review. *Journal of Speech, Language, and Hearing Research, 56,* 178–210. doi: 10.1044/1092-4388(2012/12-0148)

Kernan, K. T., & Sabsay, S. (1996). Linguistic and cognitive ability of adults with Down syndrome and mental retardation of unknown etiology. *Journal of Communication Disorders, 29,* 401–422.

Kinder, D., Kubina, R., Marchand-Martella, N.E. (2005). Special education and direct instruction: An effective combination. *Journal of Direct Instruction, 5* (1), 8–36.

King, G., Strachan, D., Tucker, M., Duwyn, B., Desserud, S., & Shillington, M. (2009). The application of a transdisciplinary model of early intervention services. *Infants & Young Children, 22* (3), 211–223.

Kover, S. T., McDuffie, A., Abbeduto, L., & Brown, W. T. (2012). Effects of sampling context on spontaneous expressive language in males with fragile X syndrome or Down syndrome. *Journal of Speech, Language, and Hearing Research, 55,* 1022–1038. doi: 10.1044/1092-4388(2011/11-0075)

Kumin, L. (2008). *Helping children with Down syndrome communicate better: Speech and language skills for ages 6–14.* Bethesda, MD: Woodbine House.

Kumin, L. (2003). *Early communication skills for children with Down syndrome: A guide for parents and professionals.* Bethesda, MD: Woodbine House.

Kumin, L. (2006). Speech intelligibility and childhood verbal apraxia in children with Down syndrome. *Down Syndrome Research and Practice, 10* (1), 10–22.

Kumin, L., & Chapman Bahr, D. (1999). Patterns of feeding, eating, and drinking in young children with Down syndrome with oral motor concerns. *Down Syndrome Quarterly, 4* (2), 1–8.

Lambe, D., Murphy, C., & Kelly, M. E. (2015). The impact of a precision teaching intervention on the reading fluency of typically developing children. *Behavioral Interventions, 30,* 364–377. doi: 10.1002/bin.1418.

Lanfranchi, S., Carretti, B., Spano, G., & Cornoldi, C. (2009). A specific deficit in visuospatial simultaneous working memory in Down syndrome. *Journal of Intellectual Disability Research, 53* (5), 474–483. doi: 10.1111/j.1365-2788.2009.01165.x

Lanfranchi, S., Jerman, O., Pont, E. D., Alberti, A., Vianello, R. (2010). Executive function in adolescents with Down syndrome. *Journal of Intellectual Disability Research, 54* (4), 308–319. doi: 10.1111/j.1365-2788.2010.01262.x

Lanfranchi, S., Toffanin, E., Zilli, S., Panzeri, B., & Vianello, R. (2014). Memory coding in individuals with Down syndrome. *Child Neuropsychology: Journal on Normal and Abnormal Development in Childhood and Adolescence, 20* (6), 700–712. doi:10.1080/09297049.2013.856396

Langthorne, P., McGill, P., & O'Reilly, M. (2007). Incorporating "motivation" into the functional analysis of challenging behavior: On the interactive and integrative potential of the motivating operation. *Behavior Modification, 31* (4), 2007. doi: 10.1177/0145445506298424

Lauteslager, P. E. M., Vermeer, A., & Helders, P. J. M. (1998). Disturbances in the motor behavior of children with Down's syndrome: The need for a theoretical framework. *Physiotherapy, 84* (1), 5–13.

Laws, G., & Bishop, D. V. M. (2004). Verbal deficits in Down's syndrome and specific language impairment: A comparison. *International Journal of Language and Communication Disorders, 39* (4), 423–451. doi:10.1080/13682820410001681207

Laws, G., & Gunn, D. (2002). Relationships between reading, phonological skills and language development in individuals with Down syndrome: A five year follow-up study. *Reading and Writing: An Interdisciplinary Journal, 15,* 527–548.

Laws, G., & Gunn, D. (2004). Phonological memory as a predictor of language comprehension in Down syndrome: A five-year follow-up study. *Journal of Child Psychology and Psychiatry, 45* (2), 326–337.

Lee, N. R., Fidler, D. J., Blakeley-Smith, A., Daunhauer, L., Robinson, C., & Hepburn, S. L. (2011). Caregiver report of executive functioning in a population-based sample of young children with Down syndrome. *American Journal of Intellectual and Developmental Disabilities, 116* (4), 290–304. doi: 10.1352/1944-7558-116.4.290

Lee, R., McComas, J. J., & Jawor, J. (2002). The effects of differential and lag reinforcement schedules on varied verbal responding by individuals with autism. *Journal of Applied Behavior Analysis, 35* (4), 391–402.

Lim, L., Arciuli, J., Liow, S. R., & Munroe, N. (2014). Predictors of spelling ability in children with Down syndrome. *Scientific Studies of Reading, 18* (3), 173–191. doi:10.1080/10888438.2013.862247

Lindsley, O. R. (1992). Precision teaching: Discoveries and effects. *Journal of Applied Behavior Analysis, 25* (1), 51–57.

Lobo, M. A., & Galloway, J. (2008). Postural and object-oriented experiences advance early reaching, object exploration, and means-end behavior. *Child Development, 79* (6), 1869–1890.

Lof, G. L. (2007). Logic, theory, and evidence against the use of non-speech oral motor exercises to change speech sound productions. ASHA Convention Invited Presentation.

Looper, J., & Ulrich, D. A. (2010). Effect of treadmill training and supramalleolar orthosis use on motor skill development in infants with Down syndrome: A randomized clinical trial. *Physical Therapy, 90* (3), 382–390.

Lott, I. T., & Dierssen, M. (2010). Cognitive deficits and associated neurological complications in individuals with Down's syndrome. *Lancet Neurology, 9,* 623–633.

Maraj, B. K. V., Li, L., Hillman, R., Jeansonne, J. J., & Ringenbach (Robertson), S. D. (2003). Verbal and visual instruction in motor skill acquisition for persons with and without Down syndrome. *Adapted Physical Activity Quarterly, 20,* 57–69.

Marcell, M. M., Ridgeway, M. M., Sewell, D. H., & Whelan, M. L. (1995). Sentence imitation by adolescents and young adults with Down's syndrome and other intellectual disabilities. *Journal of Intellectual Disability Research, 39* (3), 215–232.

Martinez, E. M., & Pellegrini, K. (2010). Algebra and problem-solving in Down syndrome: A study with 15 teenagers. *European Journal of Special Needs Education, 25* (1), 13–29. doi: 10.1080/08856250903450814

Mazzone, L., Mugno, D., & Mazzone, D. (2004). The general movements in children with Down syndrome. *Early Human Development, 79,* 119–130. doi:10.1016/j.earlhumdev.2004.04.013

McCauley, R. J., Strand, E., Lof, G. L., Schooling, T., & Frymark, T. (2009). Evidence-based systematic review: Effects of nonspeech oral motor exercises on speech. *American Journal of Speech-Language Pathology, 18* (4), 343–360. doi 1058-0360/09/1804-0343

McCollough, D., Weber, K., Derby, K. M., & McLaughlin, T. F. (2008). The effects of Teach Your Child to Read in 100 Easy Lessons on the acquisition and generalization of reading skills with a primary student with ADHD/PI. *Child and Family Behavior Therapy, 30* (1), 61–68. doi: 10.1300/J019v30n01_05

McComas, J. J., Thompson, A., & Johnson, L. (2003). The effects of presession attention on problem behavior maintained by different reinforcers. *Journal of Applied Behavior Analysis, 36,* 297–307.

McGill, P. (1999). Establishing operations: Implications for the assessment, treatment, and prevention of problem behavior. *Journal of Applied Behavior Analysis, 32* (3), 393–418.

McWilliam, R. A. (2010). Assessing families' needs with the routines based interview. In R. A. McWilliam (Ed.). *Working with Families of Young Children with Special Needs* (pp. 27–51). New York: The Guilford Press.

Meadan, H., & Halle, J. W. (2004). Communication repair and response classes. *The Behavior Analyst Today, 5* (3), 291–303.

Melchiori, L. E., de Souza, D. G., & de Rose, J. C. (2000). Reading, equivalence, and recombination of units: A replication with students with different learning histories. Journal of Applied Behavior Analysis, 33 (1), 97–100.

Mengoni, S. E., Nash, H. M., & Hulme, C. (2014). Learning to read new words in individuals with Down syndrome: Testing the role of phonological knowledge. *Research in Developmental Disabilities, 35*, 1098–1109. http://dx.doi.org/10.1016/j.ridd.2014.01.030

Mervis, C. B., & Cardoso-Martins, C. (1984). Transition from sensorimotor stage 5 to stage 6 by Down syndrome children: A response to Gibson. *American Journal of Mental Deficiency, 89* (1), 99–102.

Mervis, C. B., & Robinson, B. F. (2000). Expressive vocabulary ability of toddlers with Williams syndrome or Down syndrome: A comparison. *Developmental Neuropsychology, 17* (1), 111–126.

Miles, S., Chapman, R., & Sindberg, H. (2006). Sampling context affects MLU in the language of adolescents with Down syndrome. *Journal of Speech, Language, and Hearing Research, 49*, 325–337.

Miller, S. E., & Marcovitch, S. (2015). Examining executive function in the second year of life: Coherence, stability, and relations to joint attention and language. *Developmental Psychology, 51* (1), 101–114. http://dx.doi.org/10.1037/a0038359

Moldavsky, M., Lev, D., & Lerman-Sagie, T. (2001). Behavioral phenotypes of genetic syndromes: A reference guide for psychiatrists. *Journal of the American Academy of Child and Adolescent Psychiatry, 40* (7), 749–761.

Moodie, A. G., Hoen, R. (1972). *Evaluation of DISTAR programs in learning assistance classes in Vancouver 1971–1972.* Vancouver, British Columbia: Vancouver Board of School Trustees, Department of Planning and Evaluation.

Morgan, M., Moni, K. B., & Jobling, A. (2004). What's it all about? Investigating reading comprehension strategies in young adults with Down syndrome. *Down Syndrome Research and Practice, 9* (2), 37–44.

Morss, J. R. (1984). Enhancement of object-permanence performance in the Down's syndrome infant. *Child: Care, Health and Development, 10,* 39–47.

Morss, J. R. (1983). Cognitive development in the Down's syndrome infant: Slow or different? *Journal of Educational Psychology, 53* (1), 40–47.

Nadel, L. (2003). Down's syndrome: A genetic disorder in biobehavioral perspective. *Genes, Brain and Behavior, 2,* 156–166.

Naess, K. B., Lyster, S. H., Hulme, C., & Melby-Lervag, M. (2011). Language and verbal short-term memory skills in children with Down syndrome: A meta-analytic review. *Research in Developmental Disabilities, 32*, 2225–2234. doi:10.1016/j.ridd.2011.05.014

Naess, K. B. (2015). Development of phonological awareness in Down syndrome: A meta-analysis and empirical study. *Developmental Psychology*. Advance online publication. http://dx. doi. org/10.1037/a0039840

Naess, K. B., Melby-Lervag, M., Hulme, C., & Lyster, S. H.(2012). Reading skills in children with Down syndrome: A meta-analytic review. *Research in Developmental Disabilities, 33,* 737–747. doi:10.1016/j.ridd.2011.09.019

Nash, H., & Heath, J. (2011). The role of vocabulary, working memory and inference making ability in reading comprehension in Down syndrome. *Research in Developmental Disabilities, 32,* 1782–1791. doi:10.1016/j.ridd.2011.03.007

Nash, H. M., & Snowling, M. J. (2008). Semantic and phonological fluency in children with Down syndrome: Atypical organization of language or less efficient retrieval strategies. *Cognitive Neuropsychology, 25* (5), 690–703. doi:10.1080/02643290802274064

Neil, N. N., & Jones, E. A. (2018). Communication intervention for individuals with Down syndrome: Systematic review and meta-analysis. *Developmental Neurorehabilitation, 1,* 1-12.

Nilholm, C. (1999). The zone of proximal development: A comparison of children with Down syndrome and typical children. *Journal of Intellectual and Developmental Disability, 24* (3), 265–279.

O'Reilly, M. F., Lacey, C., & Lancioni, G. E. (2000). Assessment of the influence of background noise on escape-maintained problem behavior and pain behavior in a child with Williams syndrome. *Journal of Applied Behavior Analysis, 33,* 511–514.

Palisano, R. J., Walter, S. D., Russell, D. J., Rosenbaum, P. L., Gémus, M., Galuppi, B. E., & Cunningham, L. (2001). Gross motor function of children with Down syndrome: Creation of motor growth curves. *Archives of Physical Medicine and Rehabilitation, 82,* 494–500.

Pasnak, C. F., & Pasnak, R. (1987). Accelerated development of object permanence in Down's syndrome infants, *Child: Care, Health and Development, 13,* 247–255.

Paterson, S. J., Girelli, L., Butterworth, B., & Karmiloff-Smith, A. (2006). Are numerical impairments syndrome specific? Evidence from Williams syndrome and Down syndrome. *Journal of Child Psychology and Psychiatry, 47* (2), 190–204. doi:10.1111/j.1469-7610.2005.01460.x

Patterson, T., Rapsey, C. M., & Glue, P. (2013). Systematic review of cognitive development across childhood in Down syndrome: Implications for treatment interventions. *Journal of Intellectual Disability Research, 57* (4), 306–318. doi: 10.1111/j.1365-2788.2012.01536.x

Pereira, K., Basso, R. P., Lindquist, A. R. R., da Silva, L. G. P., & Tudella, E. (2013). Infants with Down syndrome: Percentage and age for acquisition of gross motor skills. *Research in Developmental Disabilities, 34,* 894–901. http://dx.doi.org/10.1016/j.ridd.2012.11.021

Pretti-Frontczak, K., & Bricker, D. (2004). *An activity-based approach to early intervention* (3rd ed.). Baltimore: Brookes.

Piaget, J. (1954). *The construction of reality in the child* (translated by M. Cook). New York, NY: Basic Books.

Pitcairn, T. K., & Wishart, J. G. (1994). Reactions of young children with Down's syndrome to an impossible task. *British Journal of Developmental Psychology, 12*, 485–489.

Polišenská, K., & Kapalková, S. (2014). Language profiles in children with Down syndrome and children with language impairment: Implications for early intervention. *Research in Developmental Disabilities, 35*, 373–382.

Preus, A. (1972). Stuttering in Down's syndrome. *Scandinavian Journal of Educational Research, 16* (2–3), 89–104.

Provasi, J., Dubon, C. D., & Bloch, H. (2001). Do 9-and 12-month-olds learn means-ends relation by observing? *Infant Behavior & Development, 24*(2), 195–213.

Purser, H. R. M., & Jarrold, C. (2005). Impaired verbal short-term memory in Down syndrome reflects a capacity limitation rather than typically rapid forgetting. *Journal of Experimental Child Psychology, 91*, 1–23. doi:10.1016/j.jecp.2005.01.002

Purser, H. R. M., & Jarrold, C. (2013). Poor phonemic discrimination does not underlie poor verbal short-term memory in Down syndrome. *Journal of Experimental Child Psychology, 115*, 1–15. http://dx.doi.org/10.1016/j.jecp.2012.12.010

Randolph, B., & Burack, J. A. (2000). Visual filtering an dcovert orienting in persons with Down syndrome. *International Journal of Behavioral Development, 24* (2), 167–172.

Rast, M., & Harris, S. R. (1985). Motor control in infants with Down syndrome. *Developmental Medicine & Child Neurology, 27*, 675–685.

Rast, M., & Meltzoff, A. N. (1995). Memory and representation in young children with Down syndrome: Exploring deferred imitation and object permanence. *Development and Psychopathology, 7*, 393–407.

Ratz, C. (2013). Do students with Down syndrome have a specific learning profile for reading? *Research in Developmental Disabilities, 34*, 4504–4514. http://dx.doi.org/10.1016/j.ridd.2013.09.031

Ringenbach, S. D. R., Bonertz, C., & Maraj, B. K. V. (2014). Relatedness of auditory instruction is important for motor performance in persons with Down syndrome. *Journal on Developmental Disabilities, 20* (1), 83–90.

Roch, M., & Jarrold, C. (2012). A follow-up study on word and non-word reading skills in Down syndrome. *Journal of Communication Disorders, 45*, 121–128. doi:10.1016/j.jcomdis.2011.11.001

Roch, M., FLorit, E., & Levorato, C. (2011). Follow-up study on reading comprehension in Down's syndrome: The role of reading skills and listening comprehension. *International Journal of Language and Communication Disorders, 46* (2), 231–242. doi: 10.31009/13682822.2010/487882

Roch, M., FLorit, E., & Levorato, C. (2012). The advantage of reading over listening text comprehension in Down syndrome: What is the role of verbal memory? *Research in Developmental Disabilities, 33,* 890–899. doi:10.1016/j.ridd.2011.11.022

Rondall, J. A., Lambert, J. L., & Sohier, C. (1981). Elicited verbal and nonverbal imitation in Down's syndrome and other mentally retarded children: A replication and extension of Berry. *Language and Speech, 24* (3), 245–254.

Rutter, T., & Buckley, S. (1994). the acquisition of grammatical morphemes in children with Down's syndrome. *Down Syndrome Research and Practice, 2* (2), 76–82.

Schumaker, J., & Sherman, J. A. (1970). Training generative verb usage by imitation and reinforcement procedures. *Journal of Applied Behavior Analysis, 3* (4), 273–287.

Sella, G., Lanfranchi, S., & Zorzi, M. (2013). Enumeration skills in Down syndrome. *Research in Developmental Disabilities, 34,* 3798–3806. http://dx.doi.org/10.1016/j.ridd.2013.07.03

Silverman, W. (2007). Down syndrome: Cognitive phenotype. *Mental Retardation and Developmental Disabilities Research Reviews, 13,* 228–236. doi: 10.1002/mrdd.20156

Singer Harris, N. G., Bellugi, U., Bates, E., Jones, W., & Rossen, M. (1997). Contrasting profiles of language development in children with Williams and Down syndromes. *Developmental Neuropsychology, 13* (3), 345–370. doi:10.1080/87565649709540683

Sloper, P., Glenn, S. M., & Cunningham, C. C. (1986). The effect of intensity of training on sensori-motor development in infants with Down's syndrome. *Journal of Mental Deficiency Research, 30,* 149–162.

Smith, B. L., & Oller, D. K. (1981). Comparative study of pre-meaningful vocalizations produced by normally developing and Down's syndrome infants. *Journal of Speech and Hearing Disorders, 46,* 456–51.

Smith, B. L., & Stoel-Gammon, C. (1983). A longitudinal study of the development of stop consonant production in normal and Down's syndrome children. *Journal of Speech and Hearing Disorders, 48,* 114–118.

Spanò, M., Mercuri, E., Randò, T., Pantò, T., Gagliano, A., Henderson, S., & Guzzetta, F. (1999). Motor and perceptual-motor competence in children with Down syndrome: Variation in performance with age. *European Journal of Paediatric Neurology, 3,* 7–14.

Spender, Q., Stein, A., Dennis, J., Reilly, S., Percy, E., & Cave, D. (1996). An exploration of feeding difficulties in children with Down syndrome. *Developmental Medicine and Child Neurology, 38,* 681–694.

Stein, M., Silbert, J., & Carnine, D. (1997). *Designing effective mathematics instruction: A direct instruction approach* (3rd ed.). Upper Saddle River, NJ: Merrill Prentice Hall.

Stoel-Gammon, C. (1992). Prelinguistic vocal development: Measurement and predictions. In C. A. Ferguson, L. Menn, & C. Stoel-Gammon (Eds.), *Phonological development: Models, Research, Implications* (pp. 439–456). Timonium, MD: York Press.

Tudella, E., Pereira, K., Basso, R. P., & Savelsbergh, G. J. P. (2011). Description of the motor development of 3–12 month old infants with Down syndrome: The influence of the postural body position. *Research in Developmental Disabilities, 32*, 1514–1520. doi:10.1016/j.ridd.2011.01.046

Turner, S., Alborz, A., & Gayle, V. (2008). Predictors of academic attainments of young people with Down's syndrome. *Journal of Intellectual Disability Research, 52*, 380–392.

Uzgiris, I. C., & Hunt, J. McV. (1978). *Assessment in Infancy: Ordinal scales of Psychological Development.* Urbana: University of Illinois Press.

Van Borsel, J., & Tetnowski, J. A. (2007). Fluency disorders in genetic syndromes. *Journal of Fluency Disorders, 32*, 279–296. doi:10.1016/j.jfludis.2007.07.002

Van Borsel, J., & Vandermeulen, A. (2008). Cluttering in Down syndrome. *Folia Phoniatrica et Logopaedica, 60*, 312–317. doi: 10.1159/000170081

Van Bysterveldt, A., & Gillon, G. (2014). A descriptive study examining phonological awareness and literacy development in children with Down syndrome. *Folia Phoniatrica et Logopaedica, 66*, 48–57. doi: 10.1159/000364864

Van Bysterveldt, A., Gillon, G., Foster-Cohen, S. (2010). Integrated speech and phonological awareness intervention for pre-school children with Down syndrome. *International Journal of Language and Communication Disorders, 45* (3), 320–335. doi: 10.3109/13682820903003514

Varuzza, C., De Rose, P., Vicari, S., & Menghini, D. (2015). Writing abilities in intellectual disabilities: A comparison between Down and Williams syndrome. *Research in Developmental Disablilities, 7,* 135–142.

Vimercati, S. L., Galli, M., Stella, G. Calazzo, G., Ancillao, A., & Albertini, G. 2015). Clumsiness in fine motor tasks: Evidence from the quantitative drawing evaluation of children with Down syndrome. *Journal of Intellectual Disability Research, 59* (3), 248–256. doi: 10.1111/jir.12132

Visu-Petra, L., Benga, O., Tincas, I., & Miclea, M. (2007). Visual-spatial processing in children and adolescents with Down's syndrome: A computerized assessment of memory skills. *Journal of Intellectual Disability Research, 51* (12), 942–952. doi:10.1111.j.1365-2788.2007.01002.x

Vlachou, M., & Farrell, P. (2000). Object mastery motivation in pre-school children with and without disabilities. *Educational Psychology, 20* (2), 167–176.

Welsh, T. N., & Elliott, D. (2001). The processing speed of visual and verbal movement information by adults with and without Down syndrome. *Adapted Physical Activity Quarterly, 18*, 156–167.

Will, E., Fidler, D., & Daunhauer, L. A. (2014). Executive function and planning in early development in Down syndrome. *International Review of Research in Developmental Disabilities, 47*, 77–98. http://dx.doi.org/10.1016/B978-0-12-800278-0.00003-8

Will, E., & Hepburn, S. (2014). Applied behavior analysis for children with neurogenetic disorders. *International Review of Research in Developmental Disabilities, 49*, 1–31. http://dx.doi.org/10.1016/bs.irrdd.2015.06.004

Willatts, P. (1999). Development of means-end behavior in young infants: Pulling a support to retrieve a distant object. *Developmental Psychology, 35* (3), 651–667.

Willoughby, M. T., Kupersmidt, J. B., & Voegler-Lee, M. E. (2012). Is preschool executive function causally related to academic achievement? *Child Neuropsychology, 18* (1), 79–91. http://dx.doi.org/10.1080/09297049.2011.578572

Wilson, E. M., Green, J. R., Yunusova, Y. Y., & Moore, C. A. (2008). Task specificity in early oral motor development. *Seminars in Speech and Language, 29* (4), 257–266. doi:10.1055/s-0028-1103389

Winders, P. C. (2014). *Gross Motor Skills for Children with Down syndrome: A Guide for Parents and Professionals.* 2nd ed. Bethesda, MD: Woodbine House.

Wishart, J. G. (1993). The development of learning difficulties in children with Down's syndrome. *Journal of Intellectual Disability Research, 37*, 389–403.

Yang, Y., Conners, F. A., & Merrill, E. C. (2014). Visuo-spatial ability in individuals with Down syndrome: Is it really a strength? *Research in Developmental Disabilities, 35*, 1473–1500.

Yoder, P. J., & Warren, S. F. (2002). Effects of prelinguistic milieu teaching and parent responsivity education on dyads involving children with developmental disabilities. *Journal of Speech, Language, and Hearing Research, 45*, 1158–1174.

Young, M., Baker, J., & Martin, M. (1990). Teaching basic number skills to students with a moderate intellectual disability. *Education and Training in Mental Retardation, 25* (1), 83–93.

INDEX

ABOUT THE AUTHORS

Emily A. Jones, PhD, BCBA-D, Licensed Behavior Analyst, New York, is Associate Professor in the Department of Psychology, Queens College, and The Graduate Center, City University of New York. In her research, Dr. Jones examines interventions to improve outcomes for children with developmental disabilities and their families. Phenotypic characteristics of a given disorder inform the design of tailored interventions. This includes interventions to address social-communication, cognitive, and motor skills, as well as aspects of the intensity of intervention in children with Down syndrome. For children with autism, her research has focused on improving interventions to address joint attention skills. Her research also emphasizes the needs of family members, including siblings, with evaluations of various approaches to improve sibling relationships. Dr. Jones's research has been supported by awards from the Organization for Autism Research, Doug Flutie Jr. Foundation, and Autism Speaks and published in peer-reviewed journals.

Kathleen M. Feeley, PhD, is Professor in the College of Education, Information, and Technology and Founding Director of the Center for Community Inclusion (CCI) at Long Island University Post Campus, in Brookville, New York. Dr. Feeley has dedicated her career to examining interventions that enable children with disabilities to be successful alongside their typical peers, with a particular emphasis on addressing communication skills and implementing positive behavior interventions and supports. Her work developing effective strategies that address the phenotypic characteristics of Down syndrome has been published in peer-reviewed journals. Dr. Feeley is also the Executive Director of two technical assistance centers funded by the New York State Education Department. Her work in these centers focuses on empowering families with information that enables them to be actively engaged in their children's education. Dr. Feeley also works closely with professionals to support children with developmental disabilities in general education classrooms.